WHO KII   M000194126

After Wallace entered the house, his neighbors, the Johnstons, heard him call out twice. In "about a minute and a half" Wallace came hurrying out, saying to them: "Come and see; she has been killed."

At this news they all went into the house. Wallace led them through the back kitchen and the main kitchen and into the front sitting room, where a dreadful sight awaited them. The body of Mrs. Wallace lay stretched upon the hearth rug, her feet near the gas fire and her head towards the door. Her skull had been brutally battered in with such force as to scatter her brains about the floor. Mr. Johnston reported that Wallace appeared, all the time, "as though he was suffering from a shock. He was quiet, walking round; he did not shout, or anything like that."

WALLACE INSISTED HE HAD BEEN LURED FROM HIS HOUSE BY A PHONE CALL FROM A STRANGER CALLED QUALTROUGH. THE POLICE ARRESTED WALLACE FOR THE MURDER. FIND OUT HOW DOROTHY L. SAYERS SOLVES THIS TRUE-LIFE CRIME ... AND HOW THE JURY *REALLY* DECIDED, IN ...

More Anatomy of Murder

MORE ANATOMY OF MURDER

Famous crimes critically considered by
members of the Detection Club

DOROTHY L. SAYERS   *FRANCIS ILES*
FREEMAN WILLS CROFTS

BERKLEY BOOKS, NEW YORK

MORE ANATOMY OF MURDER

A Berkley Book / published by arrangement with
The Detection Club

PRINTING HISTORY
First published 1936 by John Lane/The Bodley Head
Berkley edition/March 1990

ISBN: 0-425-12006-6

A BERKLEY BOOK® TM 757,375
Berkley Books are published by The Berkley Publishing Group,
200 Madison Avenue, New York, New York 10016.
The name ''BERKLEY'' and the ''B'' logo
are trademarks belonging to Berkley Publishing Corporation.

PRINTED IN THE UNITED STATES OF AMERICA

10 9 8 7 6 5 4 3 2 1

Foreword

Three members of the Detection Club here offer commentaries upon an equal number of murders, some famous, others unknown to the general public. In each case the writer has not been content simply to retell the story of the crime, but has endeavoured to throw light upon it; either by revelation of new facts, or by application of psychological tests to the mind of the criminal, or by comparison of the resources of present-day investigation with those of the past.

Sir Thomas Browne provides the writers with a common viewpoint, and the book with its motto:

Tis not only the mischief of diseases, and the villany of poysons, that make an end of us; we vainly accuse the fury of Gunnes, and the new invention of death; it is in the power of every hand to destroy us, and we are beholding unto every one we meet, he doth not kill us.

31 GERRARD STREET,
   LONDON,
      August, 1936.

Contents

PART I

The Murder of Julia Wallace

by Dorothy L. Sayers

The question is not: Who did this crime? The question is: Did the prisoner do it?—or rather, to put it more accurately: Is it proved to your reasonable satisfaction and beyond all reasonable doubt that the prisoner did it? It is a fallacy to say: "If the prisoner did not do it, who did?" It is a fallacy to look at it and say: "It is very difficult to think the prisoner did not do it"; and it may be equally difficult to think the prisoner did do it. . . . Can you say, taking all this evidence as a whole . . . that you are satisfied beyond reasonable doubt that it was the hand of the prisoner, and no other hand that murdered this woman? If you are not so satisfied . . . if it is not established to your reasonable satisfaction as a matter of evidence, as a matter of fact, of legal evidence and legal proof, then it is your duty to find the prisoner not guilty.—*Mr. Justice Wright's summing-up in the trial of William Herbert Wallace.*

WHEN A CRIME has been committed, the facts may be examined from three different points of view, very carefully distinguished by the learned Judge whose words I have just quoted. The people ask at once: "Who did it?" The law never has to ask this question; it waits until the people, through their representatives, the police, have produced a tentative answer by accusing a suspect, and it then asks one question only: "Did the prisoner do it?"—which is not at all the same thing. The detective novelist, a special sort of person among the people, also asks: "Who did it?" And his professional bias also prompts him to add, and to press with peculiar interest, that further question of which the law can take no cognisance: "If the prisoner did not do it, who did?"

The people, guided by instinct and communal experience, are naturally inclined to favour the most simple and obvious explanation of the facts; also it is a relief to their minds if they can believe that the right person has been accused, convicted and put out of the way; they prefer, therefore, on the whole, that the accused person should be convicted. The detective novelist, as a class, hankers after complication and ingenuity, and is disposed to reject the obvious and acquit the accused, if possible. It is the business also of the law to acquit the accused, if possible; and having done this, the law makes an end of the matter. But the detective novelist is uneasy until he has gone further and found some new and satisfying explanation of the problem.

The case of the Wallace murder shows law and people strangely and interestingly at odds, and provides for the detective novelist an unrivalled field for speculation. William Herbert Wallace was convicted by the people and acquitted by the law; and whether he was guilty or innocent the story is of a sort that (one would think) could only have been put together by the perverted ingenuity of a detective novelist. For if he was guilty, then he was the classic contriver and alibi-monger that adorns the pages of a thousand mystery novels; and if he was innocent, then the real murderer was still more typically the classic villain of fiction. And, since law and people pronounced opposing judgments, any explanation that the novelist can suggest will have the professional merit of flouting opinion and avoiding the obvious.

As in every criminal case that comes to trial, the available facts are only such as were openly produced in court. This restricted material is that upon which people, law and novelist alike have to work. The police, indeed, and the solicitors for the defence, may have had other material at their disposal; but since they did not produce it we may suppose that it was not helpful to them; and the law had to base its decision upon the evidence given at the trial. For the purpose of this article I propose, therefore, to use only the published evidence, so as to place law, people and novelist all in the same position. This is the more easy and suitable since there was, throughout the trial, remarkably little conflict of evidence. With a few trifling exceptions the facts were admitted by both sides; the only difficulty was how to interpret them. It will be seen that there is, from first to last, no single incident which is not susceptible of at least two interpretations, according to whether one considers that the prisoner was, in fact, an innocent man caught in a trap or a guilty man pretending to have been caught in a trap. Nowhere shall we find that 'master-clue' beloved of the detective novelist, which can only lead in one direction. The problem of the Wallace murder had no key-move and ended, in fact, in stalemate.

Nothing could be more respectable, more harmless, more remote from savage violence, than the antecedents of the man who in 1931 was accused of brutally beating out his wife's brains with a poker. Born in 1878, in the Lake District, William Herbert Wallace was apprenticed to the drapery trade. At the age of twenty-three (driven, according to his own statement, by a romantic *Wanderlust*) he sailed for India to take up a post as salesman in Calcutta. Here he fell seriously ill, and, after a period of employment as advertising manager in the less trying climate of Shanghai, was forced for his health's sake to return to England. He obtained a situation in Manchester, where he interested himself in politics and was appointed Liberal Agent for the Ripon Division of the West Riding. While visiting Harrogate, in 1911, he made the acquaintance of his future wife,

and on March 24, 1913, he married her. When the war put
an end to his political work, he obtained employment as a
district agent for the Prudential Assurance Company, and
moved with his wife to Liverpool. Here they rented a small,
two-storeyed house, No. 29 Wolverton Street, in the suburb
of Anfield, and here they lived for sixteen uneventful years,
in what seemed to be, in the words of a witness, "the best
relations possible".

It is, of course, always difficult to be certain how far an
appearance of married harmony may not conceal elements
of disruption. Unless the parties attract the notice of neighbours or servants by the throwing of crockery, by loud and
abusive language, by open infidelities or by open complaints, a great deal of quiet mutual irritation may go on
without anybody's being much the wiser. The Wallaces had
no children, kept no servant but a charwoman who came in
once a week, and saw but few friends; so that, if indeed
they had any disagreements, they were better placed than
many people for keeping their troubles to themselves. A
caustic judge once expressed the opinion that, in the case
of a married couple, there was no need to look for the
motive for murder, since marriage was a motive in itself;
while a cynic once argued upon the same lines to the present writer that, who but the husband *could* want to get rid
of the wife? Since nobody else could be shown to have any
motive for murdering Mrs. Wallace, the murderer *must* be
the husband, since after all he *was* her husband, and so had
his motive ready made. After his release, Wallace wrote:

> Our days and months and years were filled with
> complete enjoyment, placid, perhaps, but with all the
> happiness of quietude and mutual interest and affec-
> tion. Neither of us cared very much for entertaining
> other people or for being entertained; we were suffi-
> cient in ourselves.

It is in that very self-sufficiency, that intimate compan-
ionship extending over days and months and years, that some

writers have discovered the hidden motive for the crime: they were too close to one another, the monotony was unendurable, the husband's nerves gave way under the silent strain and he killed his wife because he was bored with her. If there had been open quarrels, that fact would have told against the husband; equally, the fact that there were no such quarrels may be held to tell against him also. Where human nature is concerned, there can never be any certainty; it all depends on the way you look at these things.

And yet it is exceedingly rare, when a husband and wife are at odds, that nobody at all should have any knowledge of their difficulties. One might think that, at some time or other during those sixteen years, the self-control of a hopelessly irritated husband would have given way. It is quite certain that, had there been any evidence at all of domestic trouble, the prosecution would have produced it, for the sheer absence of any comprehensible motive was the weakest point in their case against Wallace. There was, at any rate, no 'eternal triangle'—no other woman and no other man; if there had been any such persons it is almost inconceivable that the researches of the police could have failed to unearth them. Nor could Wallace have had any financial motive for murdering his wife, since, though she was insured for a small sum, his accounts were in perfect order and he had a sufficient balance in the bank. We may weave what fancies we like about the situation; the *fact* remains that no evidence of motive was ever put forward for the murder of Julia Wallace by her husband or anybody else.

What evidence can we, *in fact*, produce about the relations between the Wallaces?

There is, first of all, in undisputed fact that they lived together for nearly eighteen years and had no children. What conclusion we ought to draw from this circumstance we do not know, for nothing was ever said about it. Had their married relations always been normal? We do not know; at any rate, no evidence was brought to the contrary. Did Wallace, perhaps, blame his wife for their childlessness and determine to put her out of the way so that he might marry

someone else before it was too late? It is a possibility; he
was in no position to get a divorce, and the scandal of an
irregular relation with another partner would no doubt have
prejudiced him in his employment. We can only say that
the prosecution made no suggestion of any such motive. Or
did Mrs. Wallace perhaps lay the blame on her husband and
drive him to murderous fury by taunts and insults? There
was a case in the last century—closely parallel in some respects to the Wallace case—in which that situation does
seem to have occurred; but here, there is again no evidence.
Neither William nor Julia Wallace was of strong physique,
and their means, though sufficient, were not ample; they
may have been incapable of having children, or they may,
for reasons of health or finance, have agreed to remain
childless; we do not know—all is conjecture.

In the absence of a family, what were their common interests? Here we can draw upon the evidence of the witnesses, on the evidence of Wallace himself at the time of
the trial and after, and on the evidence of Wallace's dia-
ries—of which those portions at any rate which were written
before the murder may be supposed to be fairly reliable.

In Wallace, then, we have one of those mild dabblers in
science and philosophy common among self-educated men
of a speculative turn of mind. A witness for the prosecution
described him, aptly enough, as "a man who is intellectual,
and varied in his habits of study, and that sort of thing". It
was, indeed, exactly that sort of thing. He "looked at all
things with the eyes of a naturalist"; he read and noted in
his journal the newest theories about atomic physics; he
made amateur chemical experiments in a back bedroom,
which he had fitted up as a laboratory; he strove to model
his behaviour upon the stoic precepts of Marcus Aurelius;
he was interested in music, and at the age of fifty 'took up'
the violin (in half a dozen lessons from a friend); and he
was a keen and skilful chess-player. Witnesses spoke of him
as "a placid man", "scrupulously honest", "an absolute
gentleman in every respect"; one feels that he was perhaps
a little fussy, a little pedantic, a little too fond of improving

himself and other people, and something perhaps of an old maid married.

His wife Julia was, in his own words, "an excellent pianist, no mean artist in water-colour, a fluent French scholar, and of a cultured literary taste". She was dark and small, not very robust, but apparently capable of doing the greater part of the work of their little six-roomed house. One gathers that they enjoyed country rambles and excursions together (he, the naturalist, and she, the artist); that in the evenings they sometimes went out together to a play or cinema, or enjoyed a musical evening at home (she, the pianist and he, the fiddler) in the front sitting-room that was otherwise only used for "company". True, Julia failed to appreciate the "inner significance and real meaning" of *The Master Builder*, and her husband thought this strange; but she evidently did her best to share his interests.

> When she was with me [he wrote after the trial] her passion for novelty and discovery gave me countless hours of joy in explaining, as far as I could, the great riddles of the universe. . . . As I passed from practical to theoretical science my wife tried hard to keep pace with me in the newer problems of physics. . . . The hours and hours we spent together examining specimens under the microscope.

The perfect wife, surely, and model womanly woman! Only one phrase in the diary may perhaps reveal the more trying side of womanliness:

> Nothing can ever bring her back, and however much I want her, or however much I miss her loving smiles and aimless chatter . . .

Was that aimless chatter perhaps less lovable in reality than in retrospect? But probably the plainest expression of the feeling between them is to be found in Wallace's sober entry for March 25, 1929, nearly two years before the murder:

Julia reminds me to-day it was fifteen years ago yesterday since we were married. Well, I don't think either of us regrets the step. We seem to have pulled well together, and I think we both get as much pleasure and contentment out of life as most people . . .

One feels, perhaps, that here the pupil of the stoics is controlling the pen more firmly than on some other occasions; but it is scarcely the expression of a man driven to madness by disillusionment and exasperation.

And now, having made ourselves acquainted with the principal characters, we come to the strange plot of the melodrama.

The only time I left my wife alone in our little home [wrote Wallace in a published article] was to visit the Chess Club at the City Café, to deliver my lectures [on chemistry] at the Technical College, or to attend to my insurance business. On all other occasions my wife was my inseparable companion.

Monday was one of the days on which the Liverpool Central Chess Club held its regular meetings, and accordingly, on the night of Monday, January 19, 1931, Wallace left his inseparable companion at about a quarter-past seven, in order to attend the meeting and take part in a championship competition in which his name was down to play that evening. At about 7.20 the telephone rang in the café and was answered by the waitress, who then called Mr. Beattie, the captain of the Chess Club, to come and take the message. The caller, who spoke in "a strong, rather gruff voice", asked whether Mr. Wallace was in the club. Mr. Beattie said no, he was not, but would be there presently; would the caller ring up again. The caller said, "No, I am too busy; I have got my girl's twenty-first birthday on, and I want to see Mr. Wallace on a matter of business; it is something in the nature of his business." Mr. Beattie then offered to take a message, and the caller said he wanted

Wallace to come and see him the following evening at 7.30, giving his name as "R. M. Qualtrough," and his address as "25 Menlove Gardens East, Mossley Hill."

Half an hour or so later, that is, at about a quarter to eight, Mr. Beattie saw that Wallace had come into the café and started a game of chess with a man call McCartney. "Oh, Wallace," said Mr. Beattie, "I have a message for you." "Oh, who from?" said Wallace. "From a man named Qualtrough," replied Mr. Beattie. "Qualtrough, Qualtrough," repeated Wallace. "Who is Qualtrough?" Mr. Beattie said, "Well, if you don't know, I don't," and gave the message. Wallace again said, "I don't know the chap. Where is Menlove Gardens East?" Mr. Beattie did not know, nor did another member of the club whom they consulted, but they all agreed that it was probably to be found in the same district as Menlove Avenue. Having noted down the name and address in his diary, Wallace went on to finish and win his game of chess. Nothing further seems to have been said about the mysterious message until Wallace was going home, accompanied by two other members of the club. He then asked, "Qualtrough? Have you heard of that name before?" His friend said he had only heard of one person of that name, and they then discussed the best way of getting to Menlove Gardens. Wallace said he was not sure whether he would go at all, but if he did, he would take the tram to Menlove Avenue. So ended the first act of the tragedy.

Now, whatever else is uncertain about the Wallace case, one thing is abundantly clear: that, whoever sent the telephone message from "Qualtrough", it was not a genuine message but the first deliberate step towards the commission of a crime. At the trial, Wallace was accused of having sent the message himself, by way of establishing an alibi for the Tuesday evening; he himself maintained that it was sent by an enemy, so as to lure him away from home. Any argument directed to prove or disprove the genuineness of the message is beside the point: there never was an R. M. Qualtrough; there never was a Menlove Gardens East; there never was any genuine insurance business to be transacted. Whoever sent the message was the murderer; all we have to inquire is, was "Qualtrough" Wallace, or was he somebody else?

The first interesting fact is that the message was sent from a telephone kiosk about four hundred yards from Wallace's own house, and sent at exactly the time that Wallace was due to pass that kiosk on his way to the Central Café. Counsel for the prosecution made great play with this fact.

> Assuming he [Wallace] left the house on this three minutes journey at 7.15, he could easily have been in the box by 7.18; but by a singular coincidence the man who wanted him, Qualtrough, was in that telephone box at the identical time at which Mr. Wallace might have been there, and, by another singular coincidence, was trying to ring up Mr. Wallace. . . . It was a box that he [Wallace] has used. . . . The man in the box telephoned through to the Central Café. Nobody but Wallace knew that Wallace was going to be at the café; no one. . . . The man rings up, and . . . assuming that it was the prisoner . . . no doubt disguising his voice. . . . He is asked if he will ring up later. . . . He says "No." . . . If it was Wallace, obviously he would say he could not ring up later, because he would not be there. If the man had important business, and he wanted to speak to a man he did not know, do you not think he would then want to ring up later? And remember, when he was ringing up he was four hundred yards only from the house of Mr. Wallace, and it is perfectly clear that he did not call there, and he did not leave any note there. What he did do, was to telephone up to a place where he could not know he [Wallace] was going to be—it is common ground that the man who rang up . . . was planning the murder. . . . You would have thought he would be certain to see that his message . . . would get home. . . . He does nothing of the sort. . . . He never inquires afterwards

whether Wallace came there and got his message, but he leaves the whole thing in the air.

Now this argument is curiously contradictory. At one point, counsel asks, "If the man had important business, would he not have done so-and-so?" But in the next breath he admits that the man had no important business, except crime; therefore it is clear that whatever his actions might be, they could not be such as one would expect of an innocent man making a business appointment. The question that counsel was really trying to ask was not: "Can we now believe the message genuine?" but: "Could Wallace at that time have innocently believed the message genuine?" But let us examine the whole business of the telephone call carefully, point by point; for it is the very centre of the problem.

First of all: Is it true that nobody but Wallace could possibly have known that he was going to the City Café on January 19th? It is not true. Wallace was scheduled to play a championship game that night, and the list of fixtures was openly displayed in the café where anybody might see it. The meetings of the chess club always began at about the same time—roughly 7.45. Wallace was a fairly regular attendant, and we know that he was definitely expected on the Monday, because Mr. Beattie said as much to "Qualtrough". Therefore, any frequenter of the café might reasonably have looked to find him there.

Secondly: Where was the famous telephone kiosk, and what was it like? The Wallaces' house was one of a row, all having their front doors upon Wolverton Street and their back doors upon a lane running roughly parallel to the street. At a point some four hundred yards from No. 29 street and lane converged, and at this strategic point stood the kiosk—a dim little erection, lit only by the reflected rays of a street-lamp. Whether Wallace left his house by the front or the back door, he was bound to pass the kiosk on the way to the Central Café. Equally, anybody who wanted to know whether he was going to the Central Café that night had only to stand at the corner of the two streets and see whether he passed the kiosk. Thus counsel's "coincidence" turns out to be no coincidence at all, for if "Qualtrough" was not Wallace, then he must have been watching in or near the kiosk to make sure that Wallace went to the café, and, having made sure, he telephoned.

Is there anything that might indicate whether "Qualtrough" was Wallace or somebody else? There is the curious evidence of the girl at the telephone exchange. She was spoken to by the caller, who said: "Operator, I have pressed button A, but have not had any correspondent yet." She then connected him and thought no more about it. Now, counsel drew attention to the fact that Wallace often spoke from that call-box; he should, therefore, have known how to use it. But the whole point of button A's existence is that you should *not* press button A *until* you have heard your "correspondent" speak. Either, then, "Qualtrough" was unfamiliar with a public call-box, or he was too much agitated to remember the procedure. Whoever he was, he may well have been agitated: but the more usual mistake with button A is to forget to press it at all. The point is a trifling one; but, such as it is, it tells, perhaps, slightly in Wallace's favour.

Now comes the question why "Qualtrough" rang up when he did. If he was Wallace, then 7.18 was obviously the only time at which he could ring up. If not, then why did he not wait till Wallace had reached the café, or deliver a note or message at the house? There can be only one answer to this: that his face, voice and handwriting were known to the Wallaces and that he did not dare to risk recognition. Still less could he ring again later in the evening. The voice might have been disguised; Mr. Beattie said that at the time it did not seem to him to be anything but a natural one, and that it "would be a great stretch of imagination" to say that it was anything like Wallace's. But supposing it was not Wallace, how could "Qualtrough" venture, in his own voice or a disguised one, on a prolonged conversation with Wallace? He would have had to answer every kind of inconvenient question: details about himself,

details about "Menlove Gardens East", details about the
mysterious "business", and he would have had to be an
uncommonly skilful liar to get through without letting Wallace smell a rat. The tale of the birthday party was a little
fishy; but the vague message sent through Mr. Beattie had
its merits, for it held out a bait of indeterminate size and
splendour.

> Seeing the name and the daughter coming of age had
> been suggested [said Wallace in court] I considered it
> might result in a policy of something like £100 endow-
> ment, or something of that nature. I did not expect it
> would be less than that.

To a man in Wallace's position, that would have been
business worth getting. Besides, if the name was not to be
found in the directory, or the address was discovered to be
non-existent, how easy to suppose that Mr. Beattie had heard
wrongly or noted the details carelessly.

All through this case one has to remember that Wallace
lived in a small way and worked for very small profits.
Nobody is more pertinacious than your small insurance
agent. He will go miles to secure a few shillings. He would
not be disconcerted by failing to find "R. M. Qualtrough"
in a list of householders; the man might be a lodger, a
domestic servant, a newcomer to the district. Wallace said
afterwards that he had not thought to look up the address
in the directory; but in any case, new streets and houses
were being run up all over the place at a great rate, and it
might have been on of those. It was nearly as certain as
death and taxation that Wallace would never rest content till
he had investigated the whole matter personally and on the
spot.

And finally, did "Qualtrough" take no steps to ascertain
that his message had "gone home"? We cannot say that.
He had only to follow Wallace to the café. Whoever he was,
he must have been a habitué of the place to have known of
Wallace's engagement to play there that night. It is possible

that he actually arrived in time to hear the message delivered. Once we admit that he must have known Wallace and the café, all the rest follows. Any explanation that fits Wallace as the murderer also fits any murderer we may like to postulate.

The stage being now set, the curtain goes up on Act II. It is preceded by a curious little interlude. At 3.30 on the following afternoon, James Edward Rothwell, a police constable, was bicycling along a street called Maiden Lane, and saw Wallace walking on the pavement.

> He was dressed in a tweed suit and a light fawn raincoat. His face was haggard and drawn, and he seemed very distressed. He was dabbing his eye with his coat-sleeve, and he appeared to me as if he had been crying.

It was suggested to P.C. Rothwell that Wallace's eyes might have been merely watering from the cold, but the constable stuck to his opinion. On the other hand, we have the evidence of three women upon whom Wallace called between 3.30 and 5.45 to collect their insurance, that he seemed "calm" and "just as usual", that he cracked jokes with one and enjoyed a cup of tea with another. Whether the constable or the ladies were the better qualified to detect signs of emotion in an insurance agent is a question. Women are said to be observant by nature, and policemen should be observant by profession. The one certain fact is that, on that morning and afternoon of Tuesday, January 29th, Wallace transacted all his business in his ordinary accurate manner.

He stopped collecting, by his own account, at a few minutes to six and then went home for his tea. And it is now that we come to the one serious conflict of evidence in the whole case. Some time between 6.30 and 6.45 the milk-boy called with the milk; Mrs. Wallace took it in, and that is the last occasion on which she was seen alive by any disinterested person. The milk-boy, Alan Croxton Close, was 14 years old, and in his evidence he said he knew he delivered the milk at 6.30, because when he passed Holy Trinity Church it was 6.25, and it took him five minutes to get from there to 29 Wolverton Street.

On the other hand, Allison Wildman, aged 16, who was delivering a newspaper at No. 27, next door, said she got there at 6.43, and that when she had delivered her paper and gone, Close was still standing at the door of No. 29. She, too, relied on Holy Trinity Church clock. Moreover, she was seen by some boys leaving Wolverton Street some minutes after 6.40. Further doubt was thrown on Close's evidence by a number of other little boys who maintained that on the day after the murder he had told them, "I saw Mrs. Wallace at a quarter to seven"; and it was rather suggested that young Close had altered his opinion to fit the police case against Wallace. It is a close thing—a matter of five or eight minutes—the kind of point on which nobody but the characters in a detective novel can reasonably be expected to be accurate; its importance (just as in a detective story) lies in the fact that, if Mrs. Wallace was alive at 6.45 it was almost impossible that Wallace could have murdered her; for at 7.10 at the very latest he was changing trams at the junction of Smithdown Road and Lodge Lane, a good twenty minutes' ride from his home. To commit the murder between 6.30 and 6.50 would have been pretty quick work; to commit it between 6.45 and 6.50 would have been something like a conjuring trick.

Wallace stated that he left the house that evening by the back door. This, he explained, was his usual custom in the early part of the evening.

> If I was going out after six, and I knew I was going to be out an hour or two, I might go out by the back door and ask my wife to come down and bolt it after me, and on my return come in by the front door, because I would have my key.

This seems reasonable; we get the picture of the front door with its patent lock and the backyard door with its

builder's lock and iron bolts, which (and this must be borne
in mind) the householder would *expect* to find bolted against
him on his return. Mrs. Wallace, on this occasion, accompanied her husband—or so he said—by way of the back as
far as the backyard gate and there he left her, with instructions to bolt the door after him.

Now, if "Qualtrough" was lurking about the telephone
kiosk at ten minutes to seven on that dark January night,
what might he have seen? In the light of the adjacent street-
lamp he would have seen Wallace's slight figure, dressed,
not in the fawn raincoat (for the weather had cleared), but
in an overcoat, come briskly up from the back lane towards
the tramway stop. That would have been his cue that the
coast was clear at No. 29, and that his dupe was out of the
way for a good hour at least. Now would be his moment
for going to the house. If, by any chance, Mrs. Wallace had
somebody with her, he could still make some excuse and
withdraw; but if she was alone, the path to crime lay open.

Nobody (except the not impossible "Qualtrough") seems
to have seen Wallace at this stage of his journey. He is next
heard of some time between 7.6 and 7.10, at the tram-
junction at Smithtown Road, asking the conductor, one
Thomas Charles Phillips, whether the tram went from there
to Menlove Gardens East. Phillips replied, "No, you can
get on No. 5, 5A, 5W or a No. 7 car." There was nothing
in this to suggest to Wallace that Menlove Gardens East
might not exist, so he got on, observing that he was a
stranger in the district and had important business at Menlove Gardens East. Later, while paying his fare, he re-
minded the conductor that he wanted to be put off at
Menlove Gardens East, and a little later mentioned his des-
tination for the third time and was told to change at Penny
Lane. When they got there, Phillips shouted "Menlove Gardens, change here," and saw his fussy passenger sprinting
to catch the No. 7 car, which went to Calderstone. The time
was then 7.15.

On the Calderstone car, Wallace again anxiously asked
the conductor to put him off at Menlove Gardens East. Ac-

cordingly, he was put off at Menlove Gardens West, the conductor saying to him, "You will probably find Menlove Gardens East in that direction." Wallace replied, "Thank you; I am a complete stranger round here."

Now, it was said afterwards that these persistent inquiries and repeated asseverations that he was a stranger in the district and had important business there, were unnatural, and showed that Wallace was eager to impress his personality upon the tram-conductors in order to establish his alibi. This may be so—though, if fussy inquiries and irrelevant personal confidences are a proof of criminal intent, then the proportion of criminals engaged daily in establishing alibis on public vehicles must be a shockingly high one.

It is interesting that he did not succeed in impressing himself upon the conductor of the first tram—the one nearest home. The early part of the alibi is obviously the most important; did he, being guilty, think it dangerous to attract attention to himself at that stage in the proceedings? Or did he, being innocent, make no inquiry, merely because he knew the way as far as Smithdown Road? We may note at this point that Wallace appears never to have tried to establish an alibi in the strict sense of the word. He never suggested, for instance, that he was already out of the house by the time the milk-boy came. A villain in a book would, one feels, not have neglected this important point; but the argument cuts both ways, since a definite statement about times may be challenged; a mere vagueness leaves the onus of proof upon the prosecution.

Next comes the evidence of Sydney Herbert Green, a clerk, who found Wallace wandering about Menlove Gardens West and looking in vain for Menlove Gardens East. Green informed him that there was no such place. Wallace then said he would try 25 Menlove Gardens West. This he did, asking the wife of the occupier whether anybody called "Qualtrough" lived there. She said no, and he went away.

Then came a complication which was very damaging to Wallace, for when he had inspected Menlove Gardens North and South he roamed along Menlove Avenue and then found

himself (by his own account unexpectedly) in a road which
he did know. Between Menlove Avenue and Allerton Road
runs Green Lane, and in Green Lane lived a Mr. Crewe,
who was a superintendent of the Prudential Assurance
Company and whom Wallace had visited on five occasions
to take violin lessons. This, said the prosecution, proved
that Wallace was lying when he said he did not know the
district. Mr. Crewe said in cross-examination that the violin
lessons had been given two years ago and always on winter
evenings after dark. There are, of course, some people who,
after passing half a dozen times along a tram-route by night
are familiar with every crossing and turning to left and right
of the route, and who never visit a house without making
themselves acquainted with all the surrounding streets. Others (of whom the present writer is one) allow themselves to
be carted incuriously from point to point, remaining in the
end as ignorant of the general topography of the district as
when they started. Wallace, if one may trust to his evidence, was of the latter sort. "How used you to go to Wool-
ton Woods with your wife?"—"I probably inquired of some
driver of a car, which car would take us there and got on
that car." A statement which, if untrue, was well invented
to square with his known behaviour on the night of the
crime. As for knowing the lay-out of Menlove Gardens, Mr.
Crewe, who had lived just round the corner for three and a
half years, said definitely in evidence that, previously to the
trial, he himself had not had any idea whether there was a
Menlove Gardens East or not.

At any rate, suggested counsel, when Wallace found himself in Green Lane, why did he not call at Mr. Crewe's
house and ask his assistance in finding "Qualtrough's" address? Wallace replied that he did; he knocked at the door
but could get no answer. Mr. Crewe was, in fact, out that
night; so that the statement was not capable of disproof.

Having failed here, Wallace met a policeman and again
inquired for Menlove Gardens East. The constable said, cat-
egorically, that there was no such place: there was Menlove
Gardens North, South and West, and Menlove Avenue, but

no Menlove Gardens East. He suggested that Wallace should try 25 Menlove Avenue (which he pointed out); Wallace thanked him and then asked where he could find a directory. The constable said he could see one at the newsagent's in Allerton Road, or at the police station or post office. Wallace then explained, "I am an insurance agent looking for a Mr. Qualtrough who rang up the club and left a message for me with my colleague to ring up [? visit] Mr. Qualtrough at 25 Menlove Gardens East." Whether this outburst of confidence was a necessary part of alibi-faking, or was merely the ordinary citizen's apologetic anxiety to justify his existence in the eyes of the police, is again a matter of interpretation. Wallace then said, "It is not 8 o'clock yet?" and the constable agreed that it was only a quarter to. The alibi again? or only a reasonable desire to know whether the newspaper shop would still be open? However that may be, it is in the shop that we next find Wallace at 8.10, searching the directory for Menlove Gardens East. In the meantime, he had apparently been looking for the post office, but could not find it. He hunted the directory for some time, and then said, "Do you know what I am looking for?" The manageress said (not unnaturally) that she did not; he then told her that he was looking for 25 Menlove Gardens East. She then assured him that there was no such place. Curiously enough, he does not seem to have mentioned the name of Qualtrough in the shop; he said that he looked for the name in the book and could not find it; and by this time he was probably convinced that, whoever Qualtrough was, he was not a householder.

It was now about 8.20, and according to Wallace himself, he was beginning to get a little alarmed. If he was innocent, this was perhaps not unnatural. There did seem to be something rather queer about "Qualtrough", and he could not but remember that there had been one or two recent burglaries in the neighbourhood of Wolverton Street, and that it was a well-known trick of burglars to lure away householders with bogus telephone messages. Further, this was a Tuesday night—the night when, as a rule, he had a good deal of the insurance money in the house. So, giving up the vain search for Qualtrough, he walked to the nearest tram-stop to begin the journey home.

In the meantime, Mr. John Sharpe Johnston, an engineer, who lived next door to the Wallaces at 31 Wolverton Street, was getting ready to go out with his wife for the evening. The two families had been neighbours for the last ten years, and knew one another, in Mrs. Johnston's own words, "as neighbours". There seems to have been no very great intimacy. In all those years Mrs. Johnston had been into No. 29 "about three times", and then only into the front sitting-room. On all three occasions Wallace had been absent, so that Mrs. Johnston had never seen the Wallaces together in their own home; nor, evidently, had the two women been accustomed to run in and out of each other's back kitchens in the informal way that neighbours sometimes fall into. Mr. Johnston had, indeed, seen the Wallaces together from time to time, and thought them "a very loving couple, very affectionate"; but he cannot have known them very well, for he had never heard Mrs. Wallace's Christian name—or, if he had, not often enough to remember what it was. Of one thing, however, the Johnstons were quite certain: they had never heard any quarrelling going on next door, though, since the houses shared a party-wall, they would have been likely to hear anything exciting that there was to be heard.

A little before 8.45 on the Tuesday evening, the Johnstons heard somebody knocking, as it might be with the fist or palm of the hand, at the Wallaces' back door. This was nothing unusual, so they paid no particular attention to it. On going out, by way of the back door, into the entry that runs parallel to Wolverton Street, they met Wallace, just coming down at an ordinary walking pace from the Breck Road end of the entry towards his own back door. To Mrs. Johnston's polite "Good evening, Mr. Wallace," he replied only with the question, "Have you heard anything unusual to-night?" Mrs. Johnston said, in some surprise, "No—why? What has happened?" To which Wallace replied: "I have been round to the front door and also to the back, and they are both fastened against me.''

It is at this point that the detective-story writer becomes exasperated with the published accounts of the case. To him the exact mechanism of locks and bolts is meat and drink, and in writing his books he makes his witnesses offer precise information on the subject, illustrating his points, if necessary, with neat diagrams. Now, in the Wallace case, we are concerned with no less than three doors and their fastenings, all of which are of the utmost importance; yet, of these, one lock only seems to have been brought into urt, and of that there is no published description, while the witnesses are maddeningly vague in their evidence, so that it is often difficult to say whether by ''lock'' they mean a mortice-lock or a safety-lock, or even the mechanism of the door *handle*; whether by ''bolt'' they mean an iron bolt, or the catch of a safety-lock; and even whether by ''back door'' they mean the kitchen door or the yard door leading to the entry. By careful piecing together of the various statements, we may, however, come to the following conclusions.

1. The front door was the one by which Wallace was accustomed to let himself in with his own key on returning home at night. From the data furnished in evidence, it seems likely that the lock was an automatic lock, though not of the ''Yale'' type; but it is clear that no key can have been left in it on the inside, as this would prevent its being opened by another key from without. It may even have been a small mortice-lock, which Wallace would lock after him, removing and carrying away the key. This door also had a bolt, which is not described. It may have been a safety-catch or a small and easily sliding bolt immediately beneath the lockplate. If it was a stiff, heavy or double bolt, then one suggestion that was made becomes quite incredible, as will be seen. It is really extraordinary that so few details should have been reported about this bolt.

2. The back *kitchen* door seems to have had a handle, a bolt or bolts, and possibly also a lock. The mechanism of the handle seems to have been stiff and faulty.

3. The back *yard* door had apparently a latch and a bolt.
It is not perfectly clear from the evidence whether it was
this door or the back kitchen door which Wallace expected
his wife to have bolted after him when he left; he apparently
contradicted himself a little about this, but no energetic effort seems to have been made to clear the matter up.

In any case, when Wallace told the Johnstons that both
doors were fastened against him, they were "all standing
in the entry before the door into the entry had been
opened". As to what followed, let us look first at Mr. Johnston's evidence as given at the trial:

> What did you say to him then?—I suggested that he
> tried the door again, as if it was the back door, and if
> he could not open it, I would get the key of my back
> door and try.

[By a process of deduction, we may see what Mr. Johnston had in his mind. Here was no question of a Yale lock,
for which another person's key would be useless; and it
would be equally useless to try to open an ordinary lock
from outside if the key had been left in the lock *inside*.
Therefore, he must have thought that Mrs. Wallace had gone
out by the back and taken the key with her.]

> When you said, "Try again" and you would see,
> what did he do?—He went up to the door.

[Apparently the back door of the house; see later.]

> Did Mr. Wallace say anything when he went in, or
> when he went up the yard?—When he got to the door,
> he called out, "It opens now."

[Mrs. Johnston's evidence here interestingly supplements
her husband's. She remembered that Wallace, as he crossed
the yard, looked back over his shoulder and said: "She
(meaning his wife) will not have gone out; she has such a

bad cold.'' Here we have then, Wallace answering, and re-
butting, Mr. Johnston's unspoken assumption in the matter
of the key.]

Were you able to hear, from where you were,
whether he tried with his key or anything?—No, he did
not seem to try the key; he seemed to turn the knob in
the usual way.—And said, ''It opens now?''—Yes.

Mr. Justice Wright: Could you see?—Yes; I could
see him at the door, my lord.

To supplement this, we have Wallace's own statement
made at the police station.

I . . . then pulled out my key and went to open the
front door and found it secure and could not open it
with my key. I then went round to the back. The door
leading from the entry to the back yard was closed, but
not bolted. I went to the back door of the house and I
was unable to get in. I do not know if the door was
bolted or not; it sticks sometimes, but I think the door
was bolted, though I am not sure. . . . I tried my key
in the front door again and found the lock did not work
properly.

Putting these two statements together, it is clear that Wallace meant it to be understood that he had tried first the front
door, then the back door *of the house*, and then the front
door again, and that he met the Johnstons in the entry. It is
perhaps a little surprising to find Mr. Johnston asserting that
their conversation took place ''before the door into the entry
had been opened''. Did Wallace, then, carefully shut it behind him after his first fruitless attempt on the back door of
the house? Unless the door had a spring, and shut to of
itself, he must have done; and this does not look very much
like agitation of mind. A similar unnecessary carefulness
proved the downfall, under cross-examination, of Fox the

matricide. Curiously enough, nothing seems to have been made of this point by the prosecution.

Now, with regard to the back door of the house: nobody, except Mr. Johnston when he offered the help of his own key, seems to have suggested that it was locked at any time. Wallace said he thought at first that it was bolted, and subsequently came to the conclusion that the handle was merely stiff. At any rate, he eventually got in without using any key. And at this point we may take the evidence given subsequently by a locksmith.

> Witness produced another lock which he said was from the back kitchen door and found to be rusty. When the knob was turned, with difficulty, the spring bolt remained inside the lock and the knob returned to its former position.

The mention of the "knob" seems to show definitely that the reference is not to the lock, but to the latching mechanism operated by the door handle. This evidence gives support to the theory that Wallace, when he first tried the door, was misled by its stiffness into supposing it to be bolted when, as a matter of fact, the latch had merely stuck.

We shall have to come back later to this question about the locks. We will take up the story at the point where Wallace opened the door, as described by Mr. Johnston, and went in, leaving his neighbours in the yard. They do not seem to have noticed any light in the back kitchen (Wallace said that there was a gas-jet, reduced to a very feeble glimmer, over the sink); upstairs, however, the windows of the "middle bedroom" where the Wallaces slept, and of the "back room" which Wallace used as a workshop, were dimly lit, as though the gas had been left on, but turned down low.

After Wallace entered the house the Johnstons heard him call out twice, and shortly afterwards they saw first the light in the middle bedroom turned up full and then a match struck in "the small room at the top of the stairs". In "about a minute and a half" Wallace came hurrying out, saying to them: "Come and see; she has been killed." His manner, observed Mr. Johnston, who was a witness commendably free from any tendency to exaggerated language, "seemed a bit excited". Mrs. Johnston said he spoke "in a distressed tone, his words were very hurried, you know"— by which, as she explained, she meant "agitated".

At this news they all went into the house. Wallace led them through the back kitchen and the main kitchen, where he had already lit the gas, and into the front sitting-room, where a dreadful sight awaited them. The body of Mrs. Wallace lay stretched upon the hearth-rug, her feet near the gas-fire and her head towards the door. Her skull had been brutally battered in with such force as to scatter her brains about the floor, and her blood was splashed all around—on the carpet, on the arm-chair by the fireplace, on the violin-case lying on the seat of the chair, and on the wall behind. Mrs. Johnston cried out, "Oh, you poor darling!" and felt the dead woman's hand. It is not recorded what either of the two men said; but Mr. Johnston reported that Wallace appeared, all the time, "as though he was suffering from a shock. He was quiet, walking round; he did not shout, or anything like that."

There was plenty of light to see the grisly state of things, because, when Wallace had first gone into the house he had lit the gas in the sitting-room. He was cross-examined over and over again about his movements, and nothing could be clearer, or one might think, more natural, than the account he gave. He said that, after passing through the back kitchen, he opened the door into the main kitchen, which was where he would have expected to find his wife, if she was still sitting up. It was dark, and he lit the gas (which was sensible of him if he wanted to see where he was going), and then, matchbox in hand, he went straight upstairs to see if his wife was in the bedroom, calling to her as he went. Here he turned up the light, and, finding the room empty, searched the other rooms on that floor with the aid of his matches, and then came down again to try the front sitting-room—the last place where she might be expected to be, but the only other room in the house.

The door was closed to, and I pushed it a little open, and then I struck a match in quite the ordinary way, that I probably did every night I went into the room in the dark. I held it up, and as I held it up I could see my wife was lying there on the floor.

You told the officer that you thought she was in a fit?—That was my first impression, but it only lasted possibly a fraction of a second, because I stooped down, with the same match, and I could see there was evidence of signs of a disturbance and blood, and I saw that she had been hit.

Did you light the light?—Yes, I did.

Which light?—The one on the right-hand side near the window.

Why did you light that one?—It is the one we always use.

Now, the questions asked by the prosecution about this were directed to two points. First: Why, unless he knew beforehand that he was going to find a body on the floor, did he strike a match on the sitting-room threshold at all? He could have seen his way into the room quite well by reflected light from the kitchen. And secondly: Why did he walk round the body to light the farther of the two gas-jets, instead of the one nearest to him?

Now these, one would say, were the sort of questions that could only occur to a man who had never in his life had anything to do with gas. It is absolutely automatic with anyone who lives in a house with gas-lighting, to strike the match *at the threshold*, if he thinks he may have occasion to light the gas; so much so, that the present writer, for some time after making the change-over from gas to electricity, could seldom enter a room at night without first striking a match in the doorway or, at least, making a tentative gesture towards the pocket that held the matchbox.

Equally automatic would be the action of lighting the accustomed gas-jet; since a jet that is seldom used may easily turn out to have a clogged burner or a broken mantle, and the realization of this, though quite subconscious, is enough to inhibit entirely any recourse to that jet in an emergency.

Having lit the gas, felt his wife's hand and looked at her injuries, Wallace, as he said, saw that she was quite dead, and at once rushed out and called his friends. It is difficult to see what else he could have done; and all this part of the story seems perfectly consistent with his innocence.

Seeing that poor Mrs. Wallace was past all help, they all three went back into the kitchen, and there Wallace drew their attention to the lid of a cabinet, which appeared to have been wrenched off and was lying on the floor. Then he reached up to a shelf and took down a cash-box. Mr. Johnston asked whether anything was missing. Wallace said he thought about £4 had gone, though he could not be certain until he looked through his books.

This business of the cash-box is rather mysterious. It was presumably examined for finger-prints, but no evidence about this seems to have been given.[1] Wallace's prints would have been on it in any case, since he handled it to take it down; if there were others, we hear nothing of them. It was said, "Why, if an outside murderer had stolen the money, should he have so carefully replaced the box on the shelf?" It might, with equal force, have been asked why, if Wallace wanted to pretend that the murderer had been there, did *he* put it back? Common sense would have suggested that he should produce the appearance of as much disorder as possible. Like almost everything else in this extraordinary case the question cuts two ways. Then, how did it happen that there had been so little money in the box? Wallace's accounts were gone into very carefully at the trial, and everything he then said was found to be correct. On an ordinary Tuesday he would have had about £30 or £40 of the com-

---

[1] The point was put to Detective-Sergeant Bailey in cross-examination, but he replied vaguely, and the matter was apparently never cleared up.

pany's in his possession, ready for paying in on the Wednesday, which was the regular accounting day; on one Tuesday in each month he might have as much as £80 or £100, or even more. On this particular Tuesday, however, he had less than usual, first, because he had been laid up with influenza on the Saturday and had not made his round; secondly, because out of the £14 or so he had collected on the Monday and Tuesday (his other regular collecting-days) he had paid away about £10 10s. od., in sick benefit; thus leaving about £4. Let us see which way this evidence tells.

1. Supposing that there was an outside murderer, why did he not come on the Monday night, when he knew that Wallace was safely occupied with his chess-match?— Answer: Because his intention was to steal the insurance money, and what he wanted was to get Wallace out of the way on the *Tuesday* night, when a bigger sum would have been collected.

2. If the intention was to steal, why did not the thief select some night when both Wallace and his wife were out of the house?—Answer: Because (as Wallace said in evidence) when they were both out of the house they always took any of the company's money with them for greater safety.

3. But how could an outside murderer have known this?— Answer: If there was an outside murderer, he was obviously somebody well acquainted with Wallace and his habits, as is clear from other considerations mentioned earlier.

4. If Wallace himself was the murderer, would he not also select the Tuesday night, in order to suggest that the murderer was a thief in search of the insurance money?— Certainly he would.

5. In that case, since he *did* know and was probably the only person who *could* know that there would be less money that week than usual, why did he not postpone the crime to a day when he could stage a really impressive robbery?— This question is difficult to answer; unless, of course, Wallace had some idea that he might be called upon to make

good the loss; in which case his failure to collect on the Saturday might all be part of the plan.

It should be said at once that there was never any suggestion that Wallace himself committed the crime for money: his accounts were all in order; there was only £4 of insurance money; no private liabilities were disclosed; his wife was insured for the trifling sum of £20, and, though she had £90 in the savings-bank, Wallace's own bank balance was £152—ample for any emergency.

After looking at the cash-box Mr. Johnston suggested that Wallace should go and see if anything had been taken from upstairs. Wallace went up and came down almost at once, saying: "There is £5 in a jar they have not taken."

Mr. Johnston then went out for the police, and Mrs. Johnston went back with Wallace into the blood-bespattered sitting-room. Here, he stooped over his wife, and said, "They have finished her; look at the brains." Mrs. Johnston, not unnaturally, seems to have preferred not to look at any such thing; instead, she gazed round the room and said, "What ever have they used?"

Wallace made no suggestion about this; he got up and came round to the other side of the body and then said, "Why, what ever was she doing with her mackintosh, and my mackintosh?"

Mrs. Johnston then saw that there was a mackintosh lying, as she expressed it, "roughed up" and almost hidden under the body. (Later, a policeman with a gift for description said it was "as though it had been put in this position round the shoulder, and tucked in by the side, as though the body was a living person and you were trying to make it comfortable.") Mrs. Johnston was not quite sure whether Wallace had said "her" or "a" mackintosh; she was, however, quite positive that he ended his sentence by identifying the mackintosh as his own. Abandoning the problem of how the garment came there, the two of them then went into the kitchen. The fire was nearly out—"just a few live embers"—and Mrs. Johnston, "feeling that she must do something", relit it, with Wallace's assistance. Then, while they waited together in the kitchen, Wallace, who till then had been "quite collected", twice broke down and sobbed for a moment, with his head in his hands.

Now Mrs. Johnston offers us a little more evidence about the front door:

> A little later there was a knock at the door, I understand?—Yes.
>
> Did you try to open the door?—Yes.
>
> Were you able to?—No; it is a different lock to mine, and I think I was agitated, and I drew back and let Mr. Wallace open it.
>
> Do you know whether or not the door was bolted?— I do not.
>
> If he [Wallace] says he undid the bolt, you would not contradict him, would you?—I do not know whether he did, but I cannot remember that.

Nothing here is said about the necessity of a key to open the door from the inside: Mrs. Johnston merely attributes her failure to agitation and the fact that the lock was of another pattern from her own. Nor does it seem likely that she could have failed to notice the drawing of a heavy bolt or of a double bolt. The door, at any rate, was opened to admit a policeman; and he said that he did not hear any bolt withdrawn.

To this policeman, by name Frederick Robert Williams, Wallace said: "Something terrible has happened, officer." The policeman came in, examined the body, and then heard Wallace's account of his efforts to enter the house, at the front, at the back, at the front again—"this time I found the door was bolted"—again at the back—"this time I found it would open." Both then, and later, at the trial, Wallace asserted quite definitely and positively that the front door was actually bolted when he let P.C. Williams in, and this is one of the most extraordinary points about the case. If Wallace was innocent, then it is difficult to see why the real murderer or anybody else should have bolted the door; if

he was guilty, then, by sticking to the tale of the bolted
door (which rested on no evidence but his own), he probably did more damage to his own case than by any other
thing he said.

Leaving the matter of the bolts for a moment, let us accompany P.C. Williams on his tour of the house. Omitting
the questions of examining counsel, his story ran more or
less like this:

> In the middle bedroom the gas-jet was lit; accused
> said he changed in this room before going out and left
> the light burning. On the mantelpiece I noticed an or-
> nament from which five or six £1 notes were protrud-
> ing. Accused partly extracted the notes, and said,
> "Here is some money which has not been touched."
> I requested him to put the ornament and notes back,
> which he did.

P.C. Williams should have spoken sooner; a smear of
blood was subsequently found on one of the notes, but by
that time it was impossible to say that it had not got there
from Wallace's hands after his examination of the corpse.

> I approached a curtained recess to the right of the
> fireplace. Accused said, "My wife's clothes are there,
> they have not been touched." I looked in, and appar-
> ently they were undisturbed. In the back room which
> has been converted into a laboratory, accused said,
> "Everything seems all right here". In the bathroom
> there was a small light; accused said, "We usually have
> a light here."

So far, everything seemed to square with Wallace's story.
Next comes a very curious little circumstance, which
squares with no imaginable theory of the crime.

> We went into the front bedroom. It was in a state of
> disorder; the bed-clothes were half on the bed and half

on the floor; there were a couple of pillows lying near
the fireplace; there was a dressing-table in the room,
containing drawers and a mirror, and also a wardrobe;
the drawers of the dressing table were shut and the
drawers of the wardrobe were shut.

On the subject of the front bedroom, the published evidence is more vague and unsatisfactory even than it is about
the locks. Counsel for the defence seems to have asked the
prisoner:

> It is said that the bed in the front bedroom was
> somehow disarranged, and there were some of your
> wife's hats on it?—Yes.

[This is all we ever hear about the hats.]

> Do you know anything about that?—I do not think I
> had been in that room for probably a fortnight before
> the 20th or the 19th January.

Here the detective-story writer (and, one would think,
everybody else) would ask instantly: Did your wife often go
into the room? Were there sheets on the bed? If so, were
you, or was your wife proposing to sleep there on the night
of the 20th? Why? Did you always occupy the same room
as your wife, and if not, why not? According to Wallace,
his wife's bedroom "would look down on the yard" (i.e.
she slept in the "middle bedroom"), and, since he himself
changed his clothes in that room, the presumption is that
he occupied it with her; but the position is never made clear.
If the room was merely a spare room, then, one asks: What
is the meaning of the disorder? Would an outside thief and
murderer overlook the occupied bedroom with its five £1
notes on the mantelpiece, and make straight for the spare
room? And why should he there confine himself to ransacking the bed, either omitting to open any drawers and cup-
boards, or else carefully shutting them all up after him? And

if the murderer was Wallace, trying to present a convincing picture of a search for valuables, then why did he stage it, so absurdly, in this room rather than in the other?

It seems highly probable that the disorder in the front room had nothing to do with the murder; there is, however, a curious and interesting parallel in the case of the Gilchrist murder (Edinburgh, 1909). Here, the murderer, after battering his victim to death, made straight, not for the old lady's own bedroom where she kept her jewels in the wardrobe, but for the spare bedroom, where, disregarding various articles of value upon the dressing table, he broke open a box containing papers. In this case, however, the murderer is known to have been interrupted in the middle of his activities, and it has been suggested that some paper, and no ordinary valuable, was the real object of his search. Our detective novelist might play with two theories in this connection: (1) The rather melodramatic one that the murderer of Julia Wallace was in search of something that he had cause to believe might be found secreted under the spare room mattress; or (2), the idea that Wallace, in staging his murder, deliberately modelled his effects upon the Gilchrist case; this might explain his curious insistence in the matter of the bolted front door, and his subsequent statement that he at first believed the murderer to be still in the house.

Having searched the bedrooms, they went downstairs again. In the kitchen Wallace showed P.C. Williams the cabinet and the cash-box, and also picked up a lady's handbag from a chair, saying that it belonged to his wife. It contained a £1 note and some small change. They were then joined in the sitting-room by Police Sergeant Breslin, in whose presence Williams observed: "That looks like a mackintosh." Wallace, who was standing in the doorway, said, "Yes, it is an old one of mine," and, glancing out into the hall, added, "it usually hangs here." It was not until past 10 o'clock that the mackintosh was closely examined. By that time Superintendent Moore had arrived, and he, after hearing Wallace's story and examining the rooms and doors of the house, again asked Wallace whose

the mackintosh was. This time Wallace seemed to hesitate
in his answer, and the Superintendent pulled the mackintosh
out, saying, "Take it up and let's have a look at it. It's a
gent's mackintosh." Wallace said, "If there are two patches
on the inside it is mine," and, finding the patches, continued in the same breath, "It is mine." A great deal was
made, later, of this brief hesitation; it appears, however,
quite natural that, seeing the importance the police were
inclined to attach to the mackintosh, Wallace should have
thought it well to verify, by proof, his first general impression that the garment was his.

When the mackintosh was pulled out it was found to be
heavily spattered with blood on the right side, both inside
and out. Also—which was more remarkable—it was very
much burnt, and part of Mrs. Wallace's skirt was burnt also.
Yet the gas-fire before which she lay was not alight when
the body was found. Two theories were advanced to account
for the burning. One was that the murderer (in that case
Wallace) had tried to destroy the mackintosh by burning it
at the gas-fire and had accidentally burnt Mrs. Wallace's
skirt in the process; the other, that the fire had been alight
when the murder was committed, that Mrs. Wallace had
fallen against it and set her skirt alight, and that either she
was wearing the mackintosh at the time, or that the murderer had been wearing it and had burnt it in stooping to
turn out the gas.

In the same way, two theories were advanced to account
for the blood. Mrs. Wallace (who had a cold) might have
slipped the mackintosh loosely about her shoulders for
warmth, let the murderer in at the door, stooped down to
light the gas fire and been struck down with the mackintosh
still about her; or else, the murderer might himself have put
on the mackintosh to protect himself from bloodstains.

One thing seemed fairly clear: unless the murderer had
had some sort of protection he must have been heavily spattered and stained with blood. Now, throughout the house,
there were no signs of bloodstains (except, of course, in the
sitting-room), other than the smear on the £1 note in the

bedroom and a small clot on the lavatory pan in the bath-room, which, it was admitted, might have been dropped there by one of the numerous policemen[1] who were roam-ing about the place all night. There were no damp towels in the bathroom and no appearance that anybody had re-cently taken a bath. Nor was any blood found on Wallace, nor on any clothes belonging to him.

Next comes the question of the weapon. The charwoman, Sarah Jane Draper, gave evidence that since her visit on January 17th two objects had disappeared from the house: the kitchen poker and an iron bar that was usually kept in the sitting-room for cleaning under the gas fire. Search was made for these all about the house and yard and in every conceivable place, including the drains, along the tram route between Wolverton Street and Menlove Gardens where they or one of them might have been thrown away; but neither of them was ever found. Nor was any suggestion ever put forward why two weapons should have been used or why either of them should have been removed (unless, indeed, on the general principle of "making it more difficult"). For consider: whoever did the murder, it was to his advantage to leave the weapon in the house. There are only three rea-sons for getting rid of a weapon: (1) To conceal the fact that a murder has been committed at all; in this case no attempt was made to pretend that the death was suicide or accident. (2) To prevent identification by finger-prints; in this case finger-prints could easily have been wiped off. (3) To destroy a ready means of identification, as, for instance, where the murderer uses his own pistol or walking-stick; in this case the weapon was identified only with the house itself, and if the murderer came from outside, the use of a weapon identified with the house would assist him in throw-ing the blame on Wallace, whereas, if Wallace himself was

[1] These included a constable, a police-sergeant, a detective-sergeant, a detective-inspector and a detective-superintendent. Novelists who restrict their commission of inquiry to a "man from the Yard" and a gifted amateur are letting themselves off too easily. But it is hard work inventing names and characteristics for so many different policemen.

the murderer, by far the readiest way of fixing suspicion upon himself was to use a weapon belonging to the house *and remove it*, since its removal created a strong presumption that no weapon had been brought from outside. Whichever way one looks at it, the carrying away of the weapon (still more, two weapons) was an idiotic and entirely unnecessary error, involving the risk of discovery. Still, somebody made that error and took that risk, and since it could benefit nobody it gives us no help in solving the mystery. It seems likely that the weapon actually used was the iron bar; the poker, if it was not used to break open the cabinet, may have been lost on some other occasion, or Mrs. Draper had merely imagined the loss of a poker.

The body itself was examined by various medical witnesses, who, as usual, differed a good deal about the probable time of death. Professor MacFall, called by the prosecution, judged, from the fact that *rigor mortis* was present in the neck and upper part of the right arm when he saw the corpse at ten o'clock, that death had taken place "four hours or more" before his arrival. Since Mrs. Wallace had been seen alive by the milk-boy certainly not *earlier* than 6.30, this witness *must* have been at least half an hour out in his calculations. Dr. Pierce, also a witness for the prosecution, agreed with him in giving "about six o'clock" as the probable time of death. Prosecuting counsel at this point supplied the world with an admirable example of the folly of not letting well alone:

You say about six o'clock. What limit on either side would you give?—I would give two hours' limit on either side.

MR. JUSTICE WRIGHT (*pouncing on this admission of human fallibility*): It might have been between four and eight?—Yes, my lord.

COUNSEL (*making the best of it*): Would you say that death could not possibly have occurred after eight o'clock?—I would say definitely it could not have occurred after eight o'clock.

CROSS-EXAMINING COUNSEL (consolidating his advantage, after ascertaining that witness had omitted to apply all the tests he might have applied): When you say you think it was six o'clock, it might have been four o'clock in the afternoon or might have been eight o'clock?—And there were other factors as well.

So it follows she might have met her death at any hour within this time that night?—Yes.

From all this the detective novelist may well conclude that he ought not to allow his medical men to be too dogmatic in deducing the exact time of death from the appearance of the body. In fact, in the words of Professor Dible, F.R.C.S., who was called for the defence, "it is an enormously difficult subject, full of pitfalls". Nothing, in fact, emerged at the trial except that it was probable, on the whole, that Mrs. Wallace was murdered round about the time that Wallace left the house. This is exactly what one would expect. If Wallace did it, the only possible time was between about 6.30 and about 6.50; if anybody else did it, he would no doubt have entered the house as early as possible after Wallace's departure, so as to give himself an ample margin for retreat.

To go back to the night of the murder: Superintendent Moore, who came on the scene at 10.5, carefully examined all the doors and windows of the house, and found no signs that anyone had broken in. Having borrowed Wallace's latchkey and tried it in the front door, he found that, though it would open the door with a little trouble, the lock was defective. Wallace, when told, said, "It was not like that this morning"—though, actually, it turned out that the lock must have been out of order for some time. Wallace's first account was that the first time he tried the front door lock the key would not turn and that the second time he became convinced that the door was bolted. Superintendent Moore's account was that the key had a tendency to slip round in the lock, and "that if the key was turned beyond a certain point it would re-lock the door". At one point Wallace

adopted Superintendent Moore's explanation, and was much
criticized because this did not agree with his earlier account
of the matter.

It seems quite possible that both Wallace's accounts were
perfectly honest. When he first arrived at the house the key
may have stuck in the defective lock as he said. The second
time it may have turned too far, as it did with Superintendent Moore, and re-locked the door. Wallace, in the flus-
tered state of his mind, finding that, though the key turned,
the door would not open, may have jumped to the conclusion that the bolt had been shot between his two attempts.
As to his saying, "it was not like that this morning", that
may amount to no more than any man's natural reluctance
to admit that he can have made a conspicuous ass of himself. It is curious that he did not, apparently, on that night,
inform Superintendent Moore that the door had been actually bolted when he opened it to admit P.C. Williams.

Apparently, however, he had told P.C. Williams and he
may well have thought this enough. At the trial he said,
wearily, that he really could not remember what he *had* said
to the Superintendent. After all, when one has had to tell
the same story half a dozen times in one night, and innumerable times since then, it may be difficult to remember
exactly to which policeman one told what details of it.

We may bring down the curtain upon the third act of the
tragedy by quoting two little word-pictures of Wallace's de-
meanour on that memorable night. Professor MacFall said:

> I was very struck with it, it was abnormal. He was
> too quiet, too collected, for a person whose wife had
> been killed in that way that he described. He was not
> nearly so affected as I was myself. . . . I think he was
> smoking cigarettes most of the time. Whilst I was in
> the room, examining the body and the blood, he came
> in smoking a cigarette, and he leaned over in front of
> the sideboard and flicked the ash into a bowl upon the
> sideboard. It struck me at the time as being unnatural.

Detective Inspector Herbert Gold, who arrived on the scene at 10.30, agreed that Wallace was "cool and calm".

When I first went into the house on the night of the murder, he was sitting in the kitchen. In fact, he had the cat on his knee and was stroking the cat, and he did not look to me like a man who had just battered his wife to death.

Wallace's own comment, in an article written after the trial, was:

For forty years I had drilled myself in iron control and prided myself on never displaying an emotion outwardly in public. I trained myself to be a stoic. My griefs and joys can be as intense as those of any man, but the rule of my life has always been to give them expression only in privacy. Stoicism is so little practised to-day that when seen it is called callousness.

The Emperor Marcus Aurelius is, it would seem, not the wisest counsellor for those who may have to make their appearance before a British jury.

At about four or five o'clock on the Wednesday morning, Wallace was allowed to leave the house to sleep—supposing he could sleep—at his sister-in-law's. During twelve hours of the next day he was detained at the police station, making a statement and answering questions about his movements on the Monday and Tuesday evenings. In particular, he was told that the fateful telephone call had been put in from a call-box in the Anfield district near his own home.

The consequence of this was that on January 22nd, happening to meet Mr. Beattie, Wallace questioned him very closely about the exact time of the call, adding, most unfortunately for himself: "I have just left the police; they have cleared me."

This conversation was reported back to the police, who,

of course, pounced on it like tigers. Why should Wallace
be so much interested in the time? Why should he announce
that he was "cleared" when nobody, so far, had suggested
that he was suspected? As to the first, Wallace replied: "I
had an idea; we all have ideas; it was indiscreet of me."

Asked at the trial to amplify this cryptic remark, he explained that by this time he had realized he might be suspected and thought that, if he could ascertain from Mr.
Beattie that the call had been put through at seven, whereas
he himself did not leave his house till 7.15, it would be a
complete proof of his innocence. Thinking it over, he saw
that for him, a suspected person, to be seen talking to a
witness in the case, was an indiscretion. Yes; but *why* should
he imagine himself suspected? To which Wallace replied
that if his conversation with Mr. Beattie had been reported
he must have been followed and watched, and that this
showed clearly that he *was* suspected, a fact which he realized at the time. Looking at it from the purely common-
sense point of view, one must confess that Wallace would
have been a fool indeed *not* to realize that, in a case where
a married woman is murdered, the husband is always
the first person to be suspected. It was in fact admitted by the
police witnesses at the trial that, between the time of the
murder and of the arrest, Wallace had to be given police
protection while he was collecting his insurance money because the people in the district were hostile to him. Some
further light may be thrown on his statement, "I had ideas;
we all have ideas," by the fact that on that same January
22nd he mentioned the name of a certain man, known to
him and his wife and connected with the Prudential, who
was the object of his own suspicions. This person turned
out to have an alibi, and nothing, of course, was said about
him at the trial; but it is quite likely that he may have had
something to do with Wallace's indiscreet "ideas". On the
same occasion, Wallace mentioned the name of another
possible suspect, and, after his death in 1933, papers were
found among his belongings in which he named the murderer. Nothing, however, was discovered that definitely

pointed to the guilt of anyone else, so on February 2nd Wallace was arrested and charged, and on March 4th, at the conclusion of the police court inquiry, was sent up for trial at Liverpool Assizes.

It is not necessary to go through the trial[1] itself, since most of the important points in the evidence have already been discussed. We may, however, spend a little time in examining the theory of the prosecution as it eventually took shape in court.

The theory was that Wallace, having prepared his alibi the evening before, suggested to his wife after tea that they should have one of their customary violin practices in the front room. While she went to light the gas fire and get the music ready Wallace went upstairs and stripped himself naked, so that his clothes should not be stained with blood. He then slipped on the mackintosh, came down, and, catching his wife just as she was stooping to light the fire, struck her dead with repeated blows from the iron bar, with which he had already armed himself. Then, wiping his bare feet on the hearth rug, and perhaps making a hasty attempt to burn the incriminating mackintosh at the gas fire, he went upstairs, dressed, disarranged the front room and broke open the cabinet in the kitchen and then hurried out to catch his tram and establish his alibi, taking (for some reason or other) the bloodstained weapon with him.

As regards this part of the theory, several criticisms may occur to us. To commit a murder naked is no new idea; the thing was done by Courvoisier, who murdered Lord William Russell in 1840, and it was suspected in the case of Lizzie Borden, tried for murdering her father and stepmother in Fall River, Massachusetts, in 1892. But the mackintosh complicates the matter. It can scarcely be supposed to have been slipped on in order to take Mrs. Wallace more effectively by surprise; even if the poor woman had been

---

[1] April 22, 1931, before Mr. Justice Wright; for the Crown, Mr. E. G. Hemmerde, K.C., Recorder of Liverpool, and Mr. Leslie Walsh; for the defence, Mr. Roland Oliver, K.C., and Mr. S. Scholefield Allen.

given a preliminary warning by the startling apparition of a naked husband on the threshold, the smallness of the room would have enabled him to spring upon her before she could escape or call for assistance. The only conceivable justification for the mackintosh would be a curious prudery. That is not impossible. In the lower middle class there is no doubt many a man who would not—literally to save his life—appear mother-naked before his wife, even if he knew for certain that that astonishing sight was the last sight she was doomed ever to see in the world. Yet it seems strange that a murderer who had shown so much foresight in preparing the alibi should have allowed such a consideration to influence him. As for the suggested attempt to burn the mackintosh, a moment's thought would suggest that the proper place for that was not the gas-fire in the sitting-room, but the coal fire in the kitchen, which, at 6.30, when they had just finished tea, must have been burning cheerfully. It was stated in evidence that the mackintosh was of a material that would burn easily; an hour in the kitchen grate would probably have destroyed all but the buckle and buttons, which might easily have escaped search or identification. It is most unlikely that the burning of the mackintosh was anything but accidental, whoever committed the murder.

The second point is, of course, the witlessness of the disturbance created in the front room and elsewhere. Anybody wishing to suggest that a thief had gone upstairs would have removed the £1 notes from the middle bedroom and flung open the drawers and wardrobe as though in search for money.

The third unsatisfactory point is the time factor. It is astonishing what can be done in twenty minutes, which was the longest time possible that Wallace can have had at his disposal. Still, he must, at any rate, have washed his face, hands and feet, and that so carefully as to leave no smear of blood anywhere in the bathroom, dressed from top to toe, broken open the cabinet and rifled the cash-box and administered (again without leaving a trace) as much rough cleaning to the iron bar as would enable him to carry it away without staining anything it touched. The thorough removal of bloodstains is no very quick or easy matter, as anybody knows well who has tried to clean up the mess produced by a cut finger.

The other part of the theory brings us back to the vexed question of the locked doors. The theory was that Wallace, in order to get witnesses to his discovery of the body, pretended that he could not get in, when, in fact, he could have done so. We may, I think, dismiss any suggestion that he had in fact entered the house before encountering the Johnstons. What they heard and saw agreed very well with the estimated time of his arrival home and his account of his own actions. They heard him knocking, as he said, at the back door and, a few minutes later, met him coming down from the end of the entry as though, in the interval, he had been round to the front. If he was the murderer he would probably not risk making an actual entry, which might be observed by someone living in the street, if he was going to deny it afterwards.

Let us assume that Wallace is guilty and is endeavouring to present a picture of a murder committed by a third party. It is going to be a ticklish business—more ticklish than it appears at first sight. The proper handling of bolts and locks has in all likelihood planted more grey hairs in the heads of detective novelists and other planners of perfect murders than any other branch of this amiable study. Let us see how it must have presented itself to him—remembering that his meeting with the Johnstons was entirely fortuitous, and could not have entered into his calculations one way or the other.

First, then, the simplest way to suggest an intruder from without is, obviously, to follow the excellent example set by the wicked Elders who accused Susannah. They, it will be remembered, "opened the garden doors" and subsequently testified that an apocryphal young man had been in the garden "and opened the doors and leaped out". So, the apocryphal murderer must be supposed to have left the house by some means or other, and the most natural thing would be to make it appear that he escaped either by the front, leaving the door on the automatic lock, or by the back, leaving the door latched, or—more picturesquely— wide open as though in rapid flight. But alas! Where a murderer could get out Wallace could get in, and this would mean "discovering" the body without any witness to support him. He must, therefore, find "both doors locked against him". But he cannot *really* find them so, for two reasons: (1) because he is not skilled as the murderers of fiction in shooting inside bolts from the outside by means of strings and other gadgets, and (2) because, if he did, then by hypothesis the murderer would be still inside the house when Wallace arrived with his witnesses, and it would be exceedingly difficult to fake the hasty departure of a nonexistent murderer after the door was opened. He must, then, only *pretend* to be unable to get in, and *pretend* to suppose that the murderer might be still in the house. As a matter of fact, he did say all along that his first thought was that the murderer was still there, but that he abandoned that theory when they got in and found the house empty. Now, it is at this point that the emergence of the Johnstons from their back door must have upset the plans of a guilty Wallace most horribly. But for them he might have pretended that his knocking at the back door had disturbed the murderer, who must have then opened the kitchen door and fled while Wallace was trying the front for the second time. With the Johnstons there to see and hear anybody escaping, he could not very well put up that story.

Supposing the Johnstons had not come out, could the story have held water? The detective of fiction would say no; and for this reason: A cautious medical witness, inspecting a corpse at 9 o'clock, may find it difficult to say precisely whether the person was killed within two hours either way of 6 o'clock. But he will have no hesitation in saying whether or not death took place within the last quarter of an hour or so. "I would say definitely," said Dr. Pierce, "it could not have occurred after 8 o'clock." That being so, how could the murderer be supposed to have been occupying the time between the murder and Wallace's return? To explain such unaccountable lingering on the scene of the crime, one would have to present the picture of a thorough ransacking of the house from top to bottom; and this, as we know, was not done. But a consideration of this kind would probably not have occurred to Wallace beforehand, or perhaps to anybody except a detective novelist.

But, as things turned out, there the Johnstons were: and now what was Wallace to do about the front door? Was he still to insist that it had been bolted, put it on the bolt (if this had not been already done), and draw the Johnstons' attention to the bolt? This he certainly did not do, and it is odd that it does not seem to have occurred, either to him or to Mrs. Johnston, to verify that matter of the front door bolt while they were waiting for the police. If, on the other hand, Wallace, thinking his story over, had decided to leave the question of the bolt in a decent obscurity, it is odd that he should have persisted at the trial in asserting that it *was* bolted, when, in the meantime, the police themselves had offered him a perfectly good explanation for his inability to make the door open. Perhaps he felt that, having once told P.C. Williams the door was bolted, he had better stick to his story. Perhaps, when all is said and done, it really was bolted and he was telling the truth. The more we examine the question the more complicated it becomes, especially when we are left in such doubt as to the exact machinery of the lock.

Then again, if Wallace, having come back in the ordinary way and been unable to get in at the front, had gone round to the back and found the door locked, this ought not to have surprised or alarmed him. In the ordinary way it would be locked, since Mrs. Wallace would expect him to enter by the front. His story was that he was both surprised and alarmed. Why? Because of the queerness of the telephone call and the fact that he could see no light in the front kitchen. But if the curtains of the front kitchen window were drawn he could not have seen a light in any case, so why the alarm? To this he replied that by looking sideways

at the back kitchen window one could have seen the light
shining through from the front kitchen. Not if the door between the two kitchens was shut? Well, no. This did not
seem satisfactory. If he thought his wife was upstairs, why
did he not shout to her instead of knocking gently? Wallace
replied simply that he did not think of it. If he had been
trying to give the impression that the noise he made had
scared the murderer away, one would rather expect him to
make as much hullabaloo as possible. On the other hand,
too much hullabaloo might have brought out the neighbours. The neighbours did, in point of fact, come out for
another reason.

That Wallace's mind was confused, both at the time and
after, about the locked doors is evident. He said, for instance, that when he could get in by neither door, he at first
thought his wife might have slipped out to the post. This is
inconsistent with the statement that he thought a man was
in the house, but is not in itself unreasonable, and is supported by his remark to the Johnstons as he crossed the
yard. He might, in that case, having tried and failed at the
front door and got no answer at the back, have thought that
Mrs. Wallace had "slipped out" the back way, locking the
back door after her and taking the key. If so, it would naturally be useless to shout at her bedroom window, and he
would go round and make another attempt on the front door
while waiting for her return. And it was possibly then that
he first became really disturbed in his mind. It is not easy
to remember the exact sequence of one's actions or thoughts
in a moment of agitation. His own phrase, used in the course
of cross-examination, probably corresponds with the feelings of the normal person in such a situation: "I was both
uneasy and not uneasy, if you follow me." One has often
felt like that: vaguely worried yet able to present one's self
with a number of possible explanations, inconsistent with
one another, but all quite credible separately.

And, of course, the fact remains that both those locks
were defective, and had been so for a long time. Whether
Wallace, knowing this, used the circumstance deliberately

to throw an atmosphere of confusion about the whole case, or whether he was genuinely mistaken in supposing both or either of the doors to be fastened, it seems now impossible to say. It is pretty certain that he did not himself deliberately damage either of the locks in advance in order to support his story.

Now let us take the other side of the question. Suppose Wallace was innocent, how did the murderer get in? The answer was suggested by the defence. He presented himself at the front door and was let in by Mrs. Wallace, saying that he wanted to leave a note for Wallace or wait for his return. She had thrown Wallace's mackintosh over her shoulders before opening the front door (we know she had a slight cold at the time). She took the murderer into the front parlour (the usual place for receiving guests and strangers) and was there struck down. Her skirt caught fire. The murderer extinguished the flames with the bloodstained mackintosh, turned out fire and gas-light, bolted both doors in order to have notice of Wallace's return (?), washed his hands in the back kitchen (?), rifled the cash-box and cabinet, and departed, leaving the back door latched (and the front door still bolted?) and carrying the iron bar with him (!).

There are, of course, difficulties about this too. We know that there were several people, including the two men suspected by Wallace, whom Mrs. Wallace would readily have let in if they had called. She would also, if Wallace had told her (as he said he did) about the message from ''Qualtrough'', have let in anyone giving that name. Whoever the caller was, he was probably known to Mrs. Wallace, so that she had to be murdered lest she should identify him later. Would not the intending murderer in that case have brought his own weapon with him? We do not know that he did not. We have no evidence that the iron bar was the weapon used. We know only that it disappeared. An outside murderer might, seeing it handy, have used it in preference to his own or, more subtly, having used his own, he might have removed the iron bar for the express purpose of incriminat-

ing Wallace. In fact, the only thoroughly satisfactory reason
anybody could possibly have for taking it away would be
that it was clean and, therefore, if left behind, could *not*
incriminate Wallace. But one cannot expect (outside a detective novel) a thoroughly satisfactory reason for any person's actions.

An explanation of the iron bar's disappearance is offered
by Miss Winifred Duke in her novel, *Skin for Skin*, which
presents a reconstruction of the crime on the hypothesis that
Wallace was the murderer. She makes him conceal the bar
in his umbrella and drop it down a drain at the far end of
his tram journey, in the neighbourhood of Menlove Gardens. The only reply that can be made to this is that the
police said they had searched "everywhere", and they can
scarcely have omitted to search the Menlove Gardens district. Wallace could scarcely have carried it very far afield,
for his time-table leaves no room for such an excursion. If
the bar had been found in the neighbourhood, it would have
certainly incriminated Wallace. Since it was never found it
incriminates nobody, and such witness as it bears is slightly
in Wallace's favour. Its chief function is to darken counsel.
Indeed, the iron bar has bothered everybody who has at-
tempted to deal critically with the case.

Our alternative theory does indeed leave us with a bloodstained murderer obliged to clean himself and escape. But
whereas Wallace had twenty minutes only in which to do
everything and then travel by tram, the "other man" had
getting on for two hours and might then remove himself
inconspicuously on foot (possibly to a bicycle, or a car
parked somewhere handy). He had more time for cleaning,
and he need not appear so scrupulously clean.

Further, we are not obliged to suppose that the outside
murderer went upstairs at all. The £1 notes would then be
left unappropriated because he never went near them, and
the bathroom clean and dry because he did not wash himself
there. As for the front bedroom, the likeliest explanation of
all is that the murderer never went there and had nothing to
do with it. His ring at the door may have disturbed Mrs.

Wallace when she was engaged in turning over the bedding for some domestic purpose of her own. Perhaps she had piled the bed-clothes and pillows on the foot of the bed, and they fell off, as they usually do in such circumstances. The appearance of the room, as described, is more suggestive of some such household accident than of a search by a thief.

The trial itself occupied four days. Wallace himself made a very good witness—too good, perhaps, for a jury. He was, as ever, "cool and collected", and there is no kind of prisoner a jury dislikes so much, except, indeed, a hot and agitated one. But he impressed the judge. "When reference is made to discrepancies in his statement," said Mr. Justice Wright summing up, "I cannot help thinking it is wonderful how his statements are as lucid and consistent as they have been." Counsel for the prosecution, though as usual conspicuously fair in the general treatment of the case, perhaps helped a little to confuse the issues by arguing, from time to time, as though the defence was that "Qualtrough's" call was a genuine business inquiry, which it could not on any hypothesis have been; while Mr. Roland Oliver, in endeavouring to cast contempt upon the theory of the prosecution, asked the prisoner, absurdly enough, "Were you accustomed to play the violin naked in a mackintosh?" which again confused the issue. The defence also attacked the police vigorously for not having called the newspaper girl and the little boys who supported her testimony, going so far as to accuse them of deliberately suppressing evidence in order to give colour to their case. This may have prejudiced the jury, who commonly do not care to hear the police attacked, though the judge, while deprecating the attack, said he thought the police had committed an error of judgment. There was probably also a certain amount of prejudice arising from the evidence that had already come out in the magistrate's court, and from the general tendency to suspect married persons of murdering one another. But the chief difficulty in the way of the defence was the difficulty with which we started out: that the common man, however well he knows that his duty is to ask, "Did this man do it?" will insist on asking instead, "Who could have done it, if not this man?" It is perfectly evident, in the judge's summing-up, that he was aware of this difficulty. He summed up dead in the prisoner's favour, and again and again repeated his caution that the verdict must be given according to the evidence.

Members of the jury, you, I believe, are living more or less in this neighbourhood: I come here as a stranger . . . you must approach this matter without any preconceived notions at all. Your business here is to listen to the evidence, and to consider the evidence and nothing else. A man cannot be convicted of any crime, least of all murder, merely on probabilities . . . if you have other possibilities, a jury would not, and I believe ought not to, come to the conclusion that the charge is established. . . . The question is not: Who did this crime? The question is: Did the prisoner do it? . . . It is not a question of determining who or what sort of person other than the prisoner did the crime or could have done the crime; it is a question whether it is brought home to the prisoner, and whether it is brought home by the evidence. If every matter relied on as circumstantial is equally or substantially consistent both with the guilt or innocence of the prisoner, the multiplication of those instances may not take you any further in coming to a conclusion of guilt. . . . In conclusion I will only remind you what the question you have to determine is. The question is: Can you have any doubt that the prisoner did it? You may think: "Well, some one did it." . . . Can you say it was absolutely impossible that there was no such person [as an unknown murderer]? . . . Can you say . . . that you are satisfied beyond reasonable doubt that it was the hand of the prisoner, and no other hand, that murdered this woman? If you are not so satisfied, if it is not

proved, whatever your feelings may be . . . then it is
your duty to find the prisoner not guilty.

The jury, after an hour's retirement, found the prisoner
guilty.

The prisoner, being asked if he had anything to say,
briefly replied: "I am not guilty. I don't want to say anything else."

In passing sentence, the judge, whose summing-up had
been a most brilliant exposition of the inconclusive nature
of the evidence, pointedly omitted the customary expression
of agreement with the verdict.

It is said that, when the verdict was announced, a gasp of
surprise went round the court. On the general public, if not
on the jury, the summing-up had produced a deep impression.

Now, whatever rumours may have been going about beforehand in the neighbourhood of Wolverton Street, was the
main body of Liverpudlians at all happy about the conviction. Their extreme uneasiness led to one result which was
logical enough, no doubt, but highly unusual in this Christian country: a special Service of Intercession was held in
Liverpool Cathedral that God might guide the Court of
Criminal Appeal to a right decision when the case of Wallace came before it.

The answer to prayer might be considered spectacular.
On May 19th, the Lords of Appeal, after a two days' hearing
quashed the conviction on the ground that the evidence was
insufficient to support the verdict; this being the first time
in English legal history that a conviction for murder had
been set aside on those grounds. The phrasing of the judgment is exceedingly cautious, but, in the words of the
learned barrister to whom we owe the best and fullest study
of this extraordinary case:

The fact that the Court of Criminal Appeal decided
to quash the conviction shows how strong must have

been the views of the judges that the verdict was not
merely against the weight of evidence, but that it was
unreasonable.

Judges in this country are, indeed, exceedingly jealous of
any interference with the powers and privileges of a jury,
and will in general always uphold its verdict unless they see
very strong reason to the contrary.

The judgments of God, unlike those of earthly judges,
are, however, inscrutable. Any writer of fiction rash enough
to embellish his *dénouement* with an incident so unlikely as
a public appeal to Divine Justice must interpret the answer
according to his own theological fancy. If he believes that
the All-Just and All-Merciful declared for the innocent
through the mouths of the Lords of Appeal, the facts will
support that theory; but if he believes that the world is ruled
by an ingenious sadist, eager to wring the last ounce of
suffering out of an offending creature, he may point out that
Wallace was preserved only to suffer two years of complicated mental torture and to die at length by a far crueller
death than the hangman's rope. Like every other piece of
testimony in the Wallace case, the evidence may be interpreted both ways.

The Prudential Assurance Company, who had behaved
throughout in a very friendly way to Wallace, expressed
their full belief in his innocence by at once taking him back
and giving him a new job in their employment. It was,
however, impossible for him to continue with his work as
a collector on account of the suspicion which still clung
about him. He was, in fact, obliged to leave Liverpool and
retire to a cottage in Cheshire. The diary which he kept for
a year after his release contains many references to the re-
buffs he received from his former acquaintances, together
with expressions of his love for his wife which have every
appearance of being genuine. He seems to have spent his
spare time pottering about his garden and equipping his
home with little ingenious household gadgets, and trying
every means to fight off the appalling loneliness of spirit

which threatened to overcome him. "What I fear most is the long nights." "I seem to miss her more and more, and cannot drive the thought of her cruel end out of my mind." "There are now several daffodils in bloom, and lots of tulips coming along. How delighted dear Julia would have been, and I can only too sadly picture how lovingly she would have tended the garden."

On September 14, 1931, occurs a remarkable passage:

Just as I was going to dinner _____ stopped me, and said he wanted to talk to me for a few minutes. It was a desperately awkward position. Eventually I decided not to hear what he had to say. I told him I would talk to him some day and give him something to think about. He must realize that I suspect him of the terrible crime. I fear I let him see clearly what I thought, and it may unfortunately put him on his guard. I wonder if it is any good putting a private detective on to his track in the hope of something coming to light. I am more than half persuaded to try it.

Other allusions to the same person are made from time to time. Are we to believe them sincere? Or must we suppose that all this was part of some strange elaborate scheme for bamboozling the world through the medium of a private diary, which there was no reason to suppose that anyone was likely to see but Wallace himself? That he should have made this kind of accusation (as he did) in newspaper articles proves nothing; but the diary (which is far more restrained and convincing in style than the statements published over his signature) is another matter. One can only say that, if he was a guilty man, he kept up the pretence of innocence to himself with an extraordinary assiduity and appearance of sincerity.

On February 26, 1933, Wallace died of cancer of the kidneys. It is, of course, well known that disease affecting those organs produces very remarkable and deleterious changes in a person's character; but whether the trouble had already begun in 1931, and if so, whether it could have resulted in so strange a madness, with such a combination of cunning and bestial ferocity as the murderer of Julia Wallace displayed, is a matter for physicians to judge. So far as can be seen, Wallace showed no signs of mental or spiritual deterioration either before or after the crime.

It is interesting to compare the case of Wallace with that of the unfortunate clergyman, the Rev. J. S. Watson, who in 1869 murdered his wife under rather similar circumstances. Here, again, it was the case of a childless couple who had married for love and lived peaceably together for many years. The husband, a man of mild behaviour and considerable literary ability, suddenly seized the opportunity one afternoon, when the servant was out of the house, to batter his wife to death with exactly the same uncontrolled brutality as was used on Mrs. Wallace. But here the resemblance ends. Poor Mrs. Watson had for some time shown symptoms of melancholia and disturbance of mind; the wife was known to drink; there had been quarrels; and the husband, though at first he denied his guilt, soon after made an attempt at suicide and confessed the crime; nor, though he at first made some blundering efforts to cover up his tracks, did Watson contrive anything remotely approaching the elaborate ingenuity of the "Qualtrough" alibi. The superficial resemblances only serve to emphasize the fundamental disparity between the two cases.

Though a man apparently well-balanced may give way to sudden murderous frenzy, and may even combine that frenzy with a surprising amount of coolness and cunning, it is rare for him to show *no* premonitory or subsequent symptoms of mental disturbance. This was one of the psychological difficulties in the way of the prosecution against Wallace. Dr. MacFall gave it as his opinion that the brutality of the murder was a sign of frenzy. He was asked:

> So, if this is the work of a maniac, and Wallace is a sane man, he did not do it?—He may be sane now.
> If he has been sane all his life, and is sane now, it

would be some momentary frenzy?—The mind is very peculiar.

The fact that a man has been sane fifty-two years, and has been sane while in custody for the last three months, would rather tend to prove that he has always been sane?—Not necessarily. . . . We know very little about the private lives of persons or their thoughts.

The mind is indeed peculiar and the thoughts of the heart hidden. It is hopeless to explain the murder of Julia Wallace as the result of a momentary frenzy, whether Wallace was the criminal or another. The crime was carefully prepared in cold blood; the extraordinary ferocity of the actual assault was probably due less to frenzied savagery than to sudden alarm at the actual moment of the murder. It has, over and over again, come as a shocking surprise to murderers that their victims took so long to die and make such a mess about it; they have struck repeated blows, to make sure, confessing afterwards, "I thought she would never die"; "Who could have thought that the old man had so much blood in him?"

Before leaving the case for the consideration of those who may like to make of it a "tale for a chimney-corner", two small points ought perhaps to be mentioned. One is the statement made by a young woman at the trial that on the night of the murder she saw Wallace at about 8.40 at night "talking to a man" at the bottom of the entry to Richmond Park, near Breck Road. She did not know Wallace at all well, and he himself denied the whole episode. In all probability she was quite mistaken, nor could anything very much be made out of the story either by the prosecution or the defence; it is mentioned here only for completeness and for the sake of any suggestion it may offer for the novelist's ingenuity to work upon. The only practical step that was taken about it seems to have been that the police made an especially careful search of the waste ground in and about Richmond Park in the hope of finding the iron bar; but without success.

The second point concerns the choice of the name "Qualtrough". This name is extremely common in the Isle of Man, and should also, therefore, be pretty familiar to Liverpudlians. It might therefore seem a suspicious circumstance that Wallace should have professed never to have heard it before, but that it was apparently unknown also to Mr. Beattie, and that among Wallace's other acquaintances at the chess club only one said he had "heard it once before". Now, if one is preparing to give a false name, one will, as a rule, give a name that is exceedingly common, such as Brown or Smith, or one that is subconsciously already in one's mind for some reason or another. Since, to Manxmen, the name "Qualtrough" is apparently as familiar as "Smith" to an Englishman, it might seem reasonable to look for a murderer who either came from Man, or frequently went there for reasons of business or pleasure. On the other hand, if it could be shown that Wallace (either through the books of the Prudential or in some other connexion) had recently had the name brought to his notice, then that fact would strengthen suspicion against him, particularly in view of his categorical statement that he had never heard it before. It is a little curious that if the name was exceedingly well known in that part of Liverpool, no one should have drawn attention to the fact in evidence. The detective writer ought not, I think, to neglect that line of investigation.

There, then, the story remains, a mystery as insoluble as when the Court of Appeal decided that there was no evidence upon which to come to a conclusion. "We are not," said the Lord Chief Justice, "concerned here with suspicion, however grave, or with theories, however ingenious." But the detective novelist does, and must, concern himself with ingenious theories, and here is a case ready made for him, in which scarcely any "theory, however ingenious" could very well come amiss. It is interesting that the story should already have been handled twice by writers of fiction, and both times from the point of view that Wallace may have been guilty. Mr. George Goodchild and Mr.

C. E. Bechhofer Roberts in *The Jury Disagree* have used the case only as a basis on which to erect a story which includes fresh incidents and complications not forming part of the actual evidence, and have given it a "key-incident" solution in the recognized "detective" manner. Miss Winifred Duke, in *Skin for Skin*, has followed the facts with scrupulous exactness, concerning herself almost exclusively with the psychological problem of how Wallace might have come to do it (if he did do it) and what effect it had upon him.

With both novels, the criminal's motive may be summed-up in the cynical words of *Marriage à la Mode:*

> PALAMEDE: O, now I have found it! you dislike her
> for no other reason but that she's your wife.
> RHODOPHIL: And is not that enough?

It remains for some other writer, who does not find it "enough", or who is convinced by his study of the case that Wallace was telling the truth, or who merely prefers the more out-of-the-way solution to the more obvious one, to tell the story again, identifying "Qualtrough" with that to us unknown man whom Wallace himself named as the murderer.

BIBLIOGRAPHY

BOOKS DEALING WITH THE CASE ITSELF

The Trial of William Herbert Wallace, edited with an Introduction by W. F. Wyndham-Brown, Barrister-at-Law of the Middle Temple and of the Northern Circuit. London: Victor Gollancz, 1933.

This is the fullest account of the case available in book form. I am indebted to it for the greater part of the evidence at the trial, for the judgment on Appeal, and for the quotations taken from Wallace's diary.

Six Trials, by Winifred Duke. London: Victor Gollancz, 1934.

A clear summary of the case in brief compass, under the title: "The Perfect Murder".

NEWSPAPER REPORTS

The following may be consulted under the dates of the inquest, magistrates' inquiry, trial and appeal:
Liverpool Post and Mercury; Liverpool Daily Echo; Liverpool Weekly Post.

FICTION BASED ON THE CASE

The Jury Disagree, by George Goodchild and C. E. Bechhofer Roberts ("Ephesian"). London: Jarrolds, 1934.

Skin for Skin, by Winifred Duke. London: Victor Gollancz, 1935.

PART II

The Rattenbury Case

by Francis Iles

DEDICATED TO
WILLIAM ROUGHEAD, Esq., W.S.
MAESTRO OF CRIMINOLOGICAL ESSAYISTS

IT WAS THE women of England who hanged Mrs. Edith Thompson: or so, at any rate, it has been said.

"Away with this vamp!" they are reputed to have cried in their hearts. "Away with this wrecker of the sacred Home, which is our chief means of livelihood! Away with this blot upon our profession of Wife! We will teach all such that they had better be content with their allowance of one man apiece, or it will be the worse for them. Away, above all, with this stealer of young men, when young men are so scarce! To our daughters we owe it no less than to ourselves, and therefore we cry 'Away with her!' "

If this be true, the women of England acted only as their instincts bade them. When society is threatened, it will coalesce in one mass to crush the menace. Proust (was it Proust?) has said that in such a case society will open its ranks to include many whom normally it is unwilling to receive. In this instance many strange shoulders must have rubbed together; for in their determination to destroy anything that is out of pattern, women are more united and at the same time more ruthless than men. Moreover, here it was the institution of the Home itself that was threatened; and when that happens it is the women, not the men, who rush as one person, as if in mere self-preservation, to the defence.

However, if it was the women of England who hanged Mrs. Thompson, against all reason and all justice, then it was equally due to the women of England that Mrs. Rattenbury was saved from the gallows; for if Mrs. Thompson had not been hanged, Mrs. Rattenbury surely would have been.

It is impossible to avoid comparing these two cases; for not only the cases themselves but the characters of the two women concerned had so many points in common. The factors that are common to both cases are obvious: the points of character scarcely less so. Both women possessed that strange force and power of impressing the other sex, which derives from an egocentric neuroticism in the female. (In the male it is interesting to note the reverse is usually the case: women are more difficult to bamboozle in this particular respect—though to make up for that they are a great deal easier in other and no less fatal respects.)

Both, again, were highly-strung, excitable, and at times hysterical; both were inevitably wrapped up in themselves and their own affairs. But whereas Mrs. Rattenbury's vices were of the usual, ordinary kind which in a higher stratum of society are taken for granted, or even admired, Mrs. Thompson was Woman Herself: essential Woman, raised to a super-normal degree. (That if anything was what frightened the women of England about her. Ever feminine attribute which they saw and admired in themselves, they had to recognize in Mrs. Thompson developed to a pitch far beyond their own; in every department of their sex they were outclassed. Perhaps it was not only the women of England who were frightened, after all.)

But if the characters of these two women are comparable in some degree, the two young men whom they officially "led astray" were quite dissimilar.

Bywaters was, fundamentally, a decent lad; and it is an irony that it was his very decency which led him to murder. Dismissing the theory that his murder was committed on the spur of a momentary intolerable impulse (and anyone who has seen the knife which Bywaters carried with him that night will have difficulty in maintaining this theory: it was not the kind of knife which would sit comfortably in the pocket of even a ship's steward), one may yet believe that he had had almost to drive himself to murder, as a point of honour. For a decent man, when he feels his passion for a woman waning, will go to much greater lengths on her behalf than when his love was at its height, with some obscure idea of proving to himself as well as to her that he would not be such a cad as to fall out of love with her. A man less punctilious will not feel this impulse.

So it may have been with Bywaters; but so it certainly was not with Stoner.

For Stoner there is not very much to be said, though there is a little. His motive was, in all probability, mainly a sordid one, though we shall see that to some extent it may have been mixed. As to his character, the evidence of a relative at his trial that Stoner was "a good, honest lad and the best boy he had ever seen in his life" may be excused as an exaggeration due to *ex parte* prejudice. Stoner may not have been the worst lad in the world, but he certainly possessed his share of unpleasing points.

The Rattenburys were both Canadian by birth. Francis Mawson Rattenbury, sixty-seven years old at the time of the crime, was a retired architect. By a previous marriage he had two sons, now adult. Mrs. Rattenbury was a good-looking woman of thirty-eight. She had been married twice before. Her first husband was killed in the war; from the second she was divorced. By the latter she had a son aged thirteen who was away at school in March 1935. Mr. and Mrs. Rattenbury had a joint son, John, six years old at that date. Since his birth Mrs. Rattenbury had, in the useful phrase, not 'lived with' her husband.

In 1935 the Rattenburys were living at the Villa Madeira, Manor Road, Bournemouth, a stuffy little house which was definitely below the standard of life to which their income entitled them. It is not possible to say exactly how much that income was; but Mrs. Rattenbury in her evidence accounted for at least £1,000 a year which passed through her own hands, so that it is not unreasonable to suppose that the total income must have been anything from £1,500 to £2,000 a year.

Mr. Rattenbury himself, though not an impossible person, seems not to have been a very lovable one. He was close with money, and his wife had to lie to him freely in order to obtain the sums she wanted; though it is quite possible that she wanted too much, and wanted it for purposes of which few husbands could approve. His temper was uncertain, and there was a fair amount of bickering and quarrels. Mr. Rattenbury also talked a great deal about committing suicide; but one evening when his wife, bored by mere talk, challenged him to proceed to action in the matter, Mr. Rattenbury evidently saw the error of his words, for he blacked her eye for her. With pardonable exasperation Mrs. Rattenbury retaliated by biting the arm that struck her, and thought so highly of her black eye that she called in her doctor at midnight to attend to it and kept it in bed for three days.

The doctor's opinion, as expressed later, was that Mr. Rattenbury was "a very charming, quiet man", and it must therefore have been something of a surprise to him to see the havoc this charming, quiet man had wrought. However, he refrained, with or without an effort, from asking any questions as to what might have made the quiet charm temporarily slip, and proceeded to dress Mrs. Rattenbury's wounds. After that he gave her a quarter of a grain of morphia to quieten her (one may imagine that she needed quietening), and then went downstairs to remonstrate with the forceful sexagenarian. It appeared, however, that Mr. Rattenbury had gone back on his blow, for he had left the house still threatening suicide. The doctor, who seems to have revised his optimistic opinion of Mr. Rattenbury by this time, thought seriously enough of the incident to inform the police. (It may be worth mentioning that the quarter-grain of morphia gave Mrs. Rattenbury eight hours' sound sleep, and that when the doctor saw her the next morning she was peaceful and calm: one of those small points, so insignificant at the time, which assume an unexpected importance later.)

It is upon little snapshots such as this that an appreciation must always be based of the everyday life in a household to which murder comes later, usually as a quite unexpected visitor; but it must not be forgotten that such snapshots show the high lights only. Eyes were not being blacked in the Villa Madeira every day.

It was almost every other day, however, that the doctor was being called in. Between March 1934 and February 1935 he saw Mrs. Rattenbury at least seventy times, with fees amounting to over fifty guineas. In his evidence the doctor was a little cautious about the reasons for these visits, and many of them appear to have followed a summons due to excitability, temperament, or any other upsetting cause. Mrs. Rattenbury's motto, in fact, seems to have been: when in a tantrum, send for the doctor. She had, however, been genuinely suffering from pulmonary tuberculosis since 1932, and in that year she was sent to a nursing-home for a fortnight's observation.

This doctor was not only Mrs. Rattenbury's medical attendant for two and a half years but something of a family friend, and his is the only outside evidence we have of the conditions and temperaments at the Villa Madeira. It is interesting, therefore, to learn that Mr. Rattenbury had mentioned many times to the doctor his wish to commit suicide; so that it seems established that this "very charming, quiet man" had a definitely morbid streak in him—except, no doubt, late at night, as we shall see.

Concerning Mrs. Rattenbury the doctor sounds a little careful. His description of her temperament as "uneven" strikes one as a kindly understatement, and under pressure he amended this to "excitable"; and he attributed her sudden fits of excitement sometimes to too much alcohol and sometimes "if there were any upset or she was cross".

"So when she was cross or there was an upset, she sent

for you, did she?'' asked counsel; and the doctor agreed that ''if it was necessary'' she did so. This seems a perfect little picture of an excitable, rather silly woman, and it fits nicely with Miss Riggs' equally graphic remark that Mrs. Rattenbury ''ran about a good deal''.

However, reading between the lines of the doctor's evidence, one gathers the impression that in spite of her tantrums he liked Mrs. Rattenbury as a person, and he emphasized her devotion to her children, particularly to little John.

On the whole, however, notwithstanding a very infrequent black eye and a less infrequent tantrum or two, the relations of Mr. and Mrs. Rattenbury at this time (1934) were not unfriendly; and when asked at her trial if her married life had been happy, Mrs. Rattenbury threw out her hand and said simply: ''Like that''. At the same time she admitted frankly that she had not loved her husband and, if he had wanted his rights as a husband in March 1935, she would not have been willing to give them to him. Taking it by and large, then, married life at the Villa Madeira up till 1935 must have been, below the surface, much the same as married life in any other British villa where a lady with a temperament was living with a husband old enough to be her father.

That surface was, however, definitely different.

For one thing, the Rattenburys kept a chef, a figure that must be rare in the smaller villas of Britain. (There was no chef employed after Stoner was engaged; and one of the minor mysteries about this strange household is: Who did the cooking? Presumably Miss Irene Riggs, along with all the rest of the work of the house; but this seems a curious descent from the glory of a chef.) Another point of difference between the Villa Madeira and other villas was the amount of drink consumed.

Perhaps we begin to see here why the Rattenburys' standard of living was not up to their income. There may have been method in Mr. Rattenbury's meanness. What they saved on the rent they could spend on drink. Both Mr. and Mrs. Rattenbury had a weakness for the bottle.

Mrs. Rattenbury's preference was for cocktails and wine; and it is depressing, but at the same time illuminating, to learn that the cocktails consumed at the Villa Madeira were bought ready-made. Anyone who has sampled the usual ready-made cocktail, consisting of almost undiluted Italian vermouth, will understand why this information should be depressing. Its illumination lies in showing that Mrs. Rattenbury evidently drank cocktails for the sake of drinking cocktails and not for any finer points, such as flavour. We have no information about the wine that was drunk at the Villa Madeira, and possibly we are spared some rather hideous knowledge.

Mrs. Rattenbury did not drink steadily, but in bouts. In her own somewhat peculiar words: "My life with Mr. Rattenbury was so what you call monotonous that at times I used to take too many cocktails to bring up one's spirits— take them to excess." Mr. Rattenbury, on the other hand, stuck to whisky, and appears to have drunk it in doses as regular as they were large. "He always was jolly, late at night," said his wife of him in her evidence, and this almost casual remark is interesting. To keep up the practice over years of becoming "jolly" every night will need larger and larger quantities of whisky. By the time one is sixty-seven it will need a very large amount indeed. One may safely say, therefore, that Mr. Rattenbury was an exceptionally heavy drinker.

Besides Mr. and Mrs. Rattenbury and their small son, the only other occupant of the household in 1934 was Miss Irene Riggs, the "maid-companion"—or perhaps it should be "companion-help". Miss Riggs in any case was not quite in the position of a servant. She was on terms of intimate friendship with Mrs. Rattenbury, who called her "darling", and she found the household an "extremely pleasant" one.

Miss Riggs did, however, consider its atmosphere "just a little unusual", though she did not find it strange that Mrs. Rattenbury should have the habit of patrolling the gar-

den late at night in her pyjamas, or stay up all night long
playing the piano or the gramophone. And here Miss Riggs
artlessly voiced a profound truth of human nature. Had she
from the fastness of her own bed heard Mrs. Rattenbury
making this music downstairs in the sitting-room all night
long, Miss Riggs would doubtless have thought it very queer
indeed; but, in fact, she found it quite normal and ordinary,
"because I used to be with her". It is always the things that
other people do which are queer, never the things one does
oneself.

It is necessary to keep this truth constantly in the mind
for a proper understanding of the protagonist here (the court
regarded Mrs. Rattenbury as the protagonist in this domestic drama, although it was not her hand which wielded the
mallet, and we may as well accept the court's ruling). We
may find the things that Mrs. Rattenbury did very strange
and queer. To Mrs. Rattenbury herself they would appear
not merely ordinary but inevitable, simply because it was
she who was doing them.

Mrs. Rattenbury was a woman of some small culture—
though some of her turns of phrase were a little odd. At any
rate she had had a musical education of a sort, and between
bouts she used to compose songs, with which under the
pseudonym of "Lozanne" she had had a certain success.
She was also probably "artistic", if one could be sure what
that horrible word exactly means.

This, then, was the household which George Percy Stoner
entered in September 1934; ignorant then, no doubt, of the
terms upon which he was doing so.

Now habits, good or bad, must not be confused with
character. They are not always even a reflection of character
any more than accomplishments are. Bad habits, in fine, do
not necessarily mean a bad character.

Mrs. Rattenbury had one or two unfortunate habits, just
as she had two or three unfortunate characteristics. Her mode
of life, which she herself, of course, found perfectly
normal, caused a British judge and jury subsequently to
shudder. She, undoubtedly, was what the British lower

middle-class would call a ''bad'' woman. And calling her this, they would, in the usual wholesale way, deny her any redeeming qualities at all.

And no doubt so far as the petty vices go, the little vices of the body, we may all join in righteous condemnation of Mrs. Rattenbury. We may hold up pious hands of horror that a woman could drink too many cocktails, seduce a possibly innocent lad, smoke too many cigarettes, and all the rest of it. But these things are not the worst in the world. The personal vices, which leave any other individual untouched, are only minor ones; it is those which involve hurt, spiritual or physical, to another person that are the important ones. It may be argued, as indeed it was in court, that Mrs. Rattenbury by becoming his mistress caused definite hurt to Stoner, and we shall consider this question later. Here it is enough to say that, even if this is true, the damage done was completely unconscious; and that does make a difference.

For without in any way defending or excusing this woman and her foolishness, one must in honesty say that in the greater vices, the mean vices of the spirit, she seems to have been completely lacking. She was, on the contrary, in this respect rather fine: impulsively generous on the whole; and allowing for her temperament, unselfish; truthful; so far as one can judge, honest; and certainly kind-hearted. To sand the sugar, to overwork an underpaid apprentice, to lend money on oppressive terms, to bully the weak, to terrify the timid, to cheat one's neighbour within the law: all these things are worse than drinking too many cocktails—worse even than hiring a young lout to satisfy the urges of an over-ardent nature. So let the many citizens of credit and blameless renown, who habitually indulge these spiritual vices, think twice before they condemn the merely physical ones. (But, of course, they will not think even once.)

After all, everyone who came into contact with Mrs. Rattenbury seems to have liked her at once, and gone on liking her; and that is not only sound evidence of character but a thing that few of us can say of ourselves.

Above all, let those frigid souls who, having only feeble ones of their own, consider that all sexual promptings are a matter of deliberate choice by a vicious nature, or at least are subject to easy control, try to realize that all people are not like themselves. This is the official attitude towards all questions of sex in our Criminal Courts, and it is a regrettable one.

For it was this unkindness of Nature which was to prove fatal to Mrs. Rattenbury, and this almost alone. And it must be admitted that here Mrs. Rattenbury had bad luck. Even in a country notorious for its female frigidity, there are plenty of exceptions; but warm blood brings few of its possessors to the dock on a charge of murder.

For Mrs. Rattenbury was, to put it at its lowest, a highly-sexed woman. She was also an attractive one, and she was married to an elderly and possibly impotent husband. For six years she and her husband had occupied separate rooms. The situation must have been irksome to her. So after bearing it as long as she could, she followed the example of her betters and advertised for a chauffeur. It may be taken for granted that she looked over the applicants with a more than usually critical eye.

The successful candidate for this dual post was George Percy Stoner, a youth of seventeen and a half, lustier than he looked, the son of a bricklayer. Whether or no Stoner intentionally deceived Mrs. Rattenbury about his age, she certainly did not realize when she engaged him that he was so young. However that may be, in September 1934 young Stoner entered on his nominal duties as chauffeur, which consisted chiefly in driving the small boy to and from school every day, at a salary of £1 a week. On November 22nd he embarked on his real job, and became Mrs. Rattenbury's lover, at no official increase in salary. Whatever his capabilities in the former rôle, there is reason to believe that in the latter he was more than satisfactory.

Stoner was a lad whose physical properties as an adult outstripped his mental ones. As a child he had been backward in everything. He could not walk until he was three;

he was anything but brilliant at his lessons, and indeed had very little schooling; his health was indifferent. As a boy he had few friends, and those younger than himself. It is significant that, at his trial, the only evidence of character called on his behalf was that of close relations, which has little value. However, it was plain that in his post at the Villa Madeira he worked hard at his new duties; for his parents noticed that by Christmas he had become much paler, his eyes sunken and his face drawn.

At first Stoner continued to sleep at home and presented himself for duty by day only. Mrs. Rattenbury would occasionally accompany John in the car to school, and there were other expeditions in these early days, including a trip to Oxford, where they stayed the night. On this occasion, however, Mrs. Rattenbury took Miss Riggs with them, as chaperon. It was the last pleasure-trip that was to come the way of poor Miss Riggs who, in the pre-Stoner period, had usually shared Mrs. Rattenbury's jaunts to London and elsewhere.

With tolerable swiftness the relations between Mrs. Rattenbury and her young chauffeur became more friendly. It is always surprising to realize, in retrospect, how short was the period during which an important development occurred, when its progress at the time seemed so leisurely and gradual. These two must have seemed to themselves quite old friends when, early in November, Stoner confided to Mrs. Rattenbury that there was something queer about his brain for which he had to take a mysterious medicine. The nature of the medicine he refused to divulge.

Here Stoner seems to have been taking a leaf out of Mrs. Rattenbury's own book. It is a symptom of the kind of temperament and mentality with which Mrs. Rattenbury was afflicted, that the chief topic of conversation on the part of the victims is themselves: their feelings, their sufferings and, by obvious implication, their own singular importance. Evidently Stoner felt that the boot should not be confined to one foot. He could play that game too.

He succeeded to a degree that must have gratified him.

Mrs. Rattenbury was duly alarmed, and questioned him closely. Under the interrogation he still refused to say what it was that he was taking for this curious malady, but assured his employer that whatever it might be he was taking it only two or three times a year and would soon have to take it no more, for the malady would in time be outgrown. This rather tame development of a promising piece of bluff may have been due to an inkling that part of Mrs. Rattenbury's alarm was not on Stoner's behalf at all but on that of little John, who was being driven to school daily by a self-confessedly queer brain, and that if he overplayed his hand he might lose his job. If so, Stoner had suspected rightly. Mrs. Rattenbury was not yet such a fool as she became later. She did, in fact, continue after this revelation to watch Stoner with some anxiety for a week or two, until reassured that, whatever this unnamed malady might be, it did not appear to be making her employee in any way abnormal.

There is a cunning about this piece of strategic counter-bluff which arouses the admiration. It may have been an unconscious lesson that Stoner had learned, but it turned the tables so completely. No doubt it was prompted by Mrs. Rattenbury's notorious horror of drugs; and if so, calculated or instinctive, it was a move which could not have been bettered. Nothing was more likely to engage Mrs. Rattenbury's shuddering interest and goodwill. There was, of course, not a word of truth in it; and it is therefore all the more amusing to note that it was this inspired invention on Stoner's part that became the groundwork on which his entire defence at the trial was subsequently based.

On November 22nd, as we have seen, Mrs. Rattenbury became Stoner's mistress. The details attending this important and fatal event in the lives of both participants are unfortunately not known to us. The usual and easy view is that wicked Mrs. Rattenbury, a woman of thirty-eight, deliberately seduced the young and innocent lad of seventeen and a half. Perhaps she did. Without doubt she had intended this *dénouement* from the first. On the other hand, perhaps not so much seduction was required. And we have no evi-

dence that Stoner, even at seventeen and a half, was innocent. The chances, for one reason and another, are probably
against it. And even if he had been inexperienced, he was
a lad of strong passions, too; and it is quite on the cards
that, even while Mrs. Rattenbury was considering how to
bring the event about, Stoner, too, was wondering whether
he might not be able to seduce this charming lady who was
plainly so much interested in him already.

There is no question of defending or condemning this
event, nor does it matter to this account whether it was,
absolutely, a good or bad thing. The important question is
not what we think about it, but what the two people concerned thought. To arrive at that we must get away from the
atmosphere of the courts, with their necessarily conventional outlook and their complete disregard of human nature
and of the difference between human beings. The court held,
as it was almost bound to hold, that Mrs. Rattenbury wick-
edly seduced Stoner, knowing it to be an evil action. The
truth probably lies in Mrs. Rattenbury's reply to the direct
question of whether it was she who had taken the initiative:
"No, I think it was mutual." Certainly Mrs. Rattenbury
(whether through moral deficiency or any other cause, does
not matter) had no idea that she was doing a deliberately
wicked thing. Equally certainly, neither she nor Stoner
would have thought that it was anything to make such a fuss
about. No doubt this was very reprehensible of both of them,
but that is how things are in the event.

After the liaison had been consummated, then, a bedroom was put at Stoner's disposal at the Villa Madeira. He
left his home and in future occupied either this bedroom or
Mrs. Rattenbury's from night to night as was the more convenient. Mr. Rattenbury, it may be said, slept downstairs.

Mr. Rattenbury, indeed, who could not have been ignorant of this arrangement, appears to have regarded it with
equanimity. Two years earlier he had told his wife to lead
her own life, and shortly after Stoner had moved into the
house Mrs. Rattenbury informed her husband that she had

taken him at his word. Mr. Rattenbury's reaction to this
engaging frankness is not recorded, but it seems that only
one person viewed the situation with disfavour. Miss Riggs,
the close friend and confidante of Mrs. Rattenbury for the
last four years, could naturally not feel enthusiastic about
being supplanted.

Mrs. Rattenbury now had things as she wanted them; and
if she had kept both her head and a firm hand on the situation, the secrets of the Villa Madeira would never have
found their way into gleeful print. But she did not. She
committed the mistake, fatal in her case, of falling in love
with Stoner.

The fatal element was Mrs. Rattenbury's generosity. In a
material way she could express her affection only by show-
ering gifts upon its object; and upon Stoner she now proceeded to shower ten-pound notes, silk pyjamas, gold
watches, and anything else for which he expressed a wish.
For a young man of Stoner's upbringing and incomplete
mental development this was the worst possible treatment.
Such unwonted lavishness undoubtedly went to his head.

It must be emphasized, however, that even so, the situation as between Mrs. Rattenbury and Stoner was, during
this incubation period from November to March, no unique
one. It is not even so very unusual. Certainly there was
nothing to show that, in this particular instance, it was
brewing up for murder.

January 1935 seems to have been a more or less peaceful
month in the Rattenbury home, so far as peace ever could
attend that storm-centre, its mistress; at all events, we hear
of no particular upsets. Stoner was being taken more and
more into the confidence of Mrs. Rattenbury, and he now
cashed all her cheques for her. At the same time he was
gaining influence over her. At his request she gave up her
cocktails altogether (surely the measure of a great love); and
his now increasing jealousy, though it irked her at times,
must on the whole have delighted her.

In February the drug *motif* crops up again.

Mrs. Rattenbury and Stoner had their quarrels. As early

as January Stoner had been heard to threaten Mrs. Rattenbury's life, though this threat was not taken very seriously by anyone. In February, however, a more serious quarrel occurred. Between eleven and twelve o'clock one night Miss Riggs, from her bedroom, heard it begin in Mrs. Rattenbury's room, continue along the passage, and progress into Stoner's bedroom. Thinking it more serious than usual, Miss Riggs got up to investigate. She found the combatants in a clinch, Stoner having obtained a "firm hold" of Mrs. Rattenbury, who was "rather scared". Miss Riggs separated them.

The cause of this quarrel is not given, but from its date and the direction of its progress one may guess that it had something to do with the efforts that Mrs. Rattenbury was making at this time to break the connection between herself and Stoner on account of the disparity in their ages. This break Stoner violently opposed. The re-introduction of the drug theme here was probably made by Stoner as a further weapon to support his case, by way of an appeal *ad misericordiam* to reinforce the appeal *ad cor*.

In any case Stoner told Mrs. Rattenbury one morning that he had to go up to London that day to obtain a further supply of his mysterious drug, and his manner was extremely agitated.

Once again the effect of this communication on Mrs. Rattenbury was all that Stoner could have hoped. Her agitation instantly rivalled his own, and she begged him not to go. Stoner, however, was the adamant young drug-fiend and went, leaving his mistress almost in hysterics. As usual when upset, Mrs. Rattenbury at once telephoned for her doctor.

On this occasion, however, she had a good excuse for doing so, for she told the doctor all about Stoner's distressing story and implored his help. The doctor promised to have a talk with Stoner.

The talk took place the next day, and Stoner admitted readily enough that it was cocaine that he was taking; he had found some lying about in the house and sampled it and

it had given him a pleasant sensation. The doctor accepted
this story, warned Stoner about the drug, and offered to help
him if he wished to give it up. It is a pity that the doctor
did not question Stoner a little more closely on this occasion, for it might have saved a lot of wasted time at the trial
had he done so. He might, for instance, have learned that
Stoner considered cocaine to be a brown powder with black
spots and that one can take a heaped-up teaspoonful of it
containing thirty-six grains with not even any unpleasant
after-effects, though the average fatal dose is fifteen grains.
The doctor, however, confined himself, in reporting the interview to Mrs. Rattenbury, to warning her with profession-
ally impersonal caution that ''if you want to stop someone
taking cocaine you would not give them more money than
you could help.''

Stoner must have come away from that interview tolerably cock-a-hoop. He knew very little about cocaine, but he
had nevertheless taken the doctor in; and with instinctive
cunning he had said that he had been unable to obtain any
in London on the previous day, and so had run no risk of
being asked to show a sample of the noxious stuff he was
taking. And though Stoner did not know it, the foundations
of his subsequent defence had now been cemented.

(It may be as well to say here that Stoner never did take
cocaine, or any similar drug. The reliable medical evidence
at the trial definitely disproved that Stoner could have been
a cocaine-addict, and Mr. Justice Humphreys made his
opinion on the point quite clear in his summing-up. The
whole story must have been made up by Stoner simply to
impress Mrs. Rattenbury. What he was taking was an aph-
rodisiac.)

From February the chain of significant events links up to
Tuesday, March 19th. On that day Mrs. Rattenbury took
Stoner with her on a jaunt to London. It is not too much to
say that it was to this visit to London that Mr. Rattenbury's
murder was directly due.

Mrs. Rattenbury and Stoner stayed, as brother and sister,
at a good hotel. Mrs. Rattenbury signed the register as

"Mrs. Rattenbury and brother"; when the clerk asked her to fill in the name of her brother, she wrote what he took to be "George Stone". March 19th was spent chiefly in shopping for Stoner. Purchases made at Harrods' included two pairs of shoes and trees, three pairs of men's *crêpe de Chine* pyjamas at 60*s.* a pair, shirts, ties, silk and linen handkerchiefs, socks, gloves, underwear, a grey suit, a blue suit, and a mackintosh. In fact Stoner did pretty well. On the same day Stoner bought Mrs. Rattenbury a present of a diamond ring for £15 10*s.,* in Bond Street. But as Mrs. Rattenbury had given him £20 for the purpose, Stoner did not do badly out of this either.

That seems to have concluded the shopping, and the next days were spent in sight-seeing, cinemas, theatres, and restaurants in the usual way. These four days of luxury, in the company of a woman who was ready to gratify every whim, completed Stoner's moral disintegration.

Mrs. Rattenbury had obtained the money for this jaunt by telling her husband that she had to go to London for an operation. It was her custom to tell some lie of this kind regularly every June and December in order to squeeze something extra out of her husband over and above her regular housekeeping and personal allowance of £600 a year; and she must have been a good liar, because she usually managed to raise another £150 or more on each of these occasions. This time she must have managed things exceptionally well, for not only was the dividend an interim one but it was much larger than usual; for Mr. Rattenbury, rendered soft no doubt by pity that his wife should have to undergo yet another operation (she had had one or two recently), parted with no less than £250.

Mrs. Rattenbury must not only have told her story well; she must have chosen her time with equal care. It is a little surprising to find a man reputedly mean handing out a sum of this size, until one remembers that in the evenings Mr. Rattenbury was "jolly". Perhaps Mrs. Rattenbury selected an evening when Mr. Rattenbury was even "jollier" than usual; for when she turned up again, hale and whole, four

days later, nothing appears to have been said about the singular speed of this operation and the patient's recovery from
it. One may assume that Mr. Rattenbury, in the extremes
of his jollity, had forgotten all about it. That he might
equally well have forgotten about the cheque, and that it
might be very much to Mrs. Rattenbury's advantage that he
should never remember, is a possible, if perhaps somewhat
academic point in favour of premeditation which does not
seem to have been made by the prosecution at the trial. In
any case, within forty-eight hours Mr. Rattenbury was to
have no chance of remembering any inconsistencies of this
sort.

Stoner and Mrs. Rattenbury returned to the Villa Madeira
at half-past ten on Friday evening, March 22nd. Mr. Rattenbury was in bed, jolly, and asked no questions.

On the Saturday morning Mrs. Rattenbury went with
Stoner in the car to collect her small son from school, as
he was to come home for the week-end. (He was a day-boy
when Stoner was first engaged, but we hear of him now as
a boarder.) In the afternoon Stoner drove Mrs. Rattenbury
and the little boy over to watch Mrs. Rattenbury's elder son
playing football at his school. Mr. Rattenbury stayed at
home. The evening passed quietly, with Mr. and Mrs. Rattenbury playing cards together; "just the same as any other
night", except that it happened to be Mr. Rattenbury's last
on earth.

On Sunday Mr. Rattenbury was depressed. He was interested financially in a block of flats that was being built at
Southampton, and the investment was worrying him. To
cheer him up Mrs. Rattenbury took him for a drive in the
morning and was particularly nice to him, but Mr. Rattenbury's gloom remained. After lunch Mr. Rattenbury went
to sleep, and Mrs. Rattenbury played with John: "the usual
Sunday afternoon". The three of them had tea in Mrs. Rattenbury's bedroom. Miss Riggs was out for the afternoon
and evening, and Stoner brought up the tea, as apparently
was not unusual.

The door of the bedroom was normally ajar, with a clothes-basket to wedge it open. Shortly after Stoner had brought the tea somebody, probably the little boy, moved the basket and the door remained shut for a time.

After tea the trio moved down to the drawing-room, little John was in and out, and Mr. Rattenbury was engaged with a book. Some mystery was made about this book at the trial, and Mrs. Rattenbury's *résumé* of its story was as follows: "The person in the book said he had lived too long and, before he became doddering, as far as I can understand, he finished himself." This project appealed to Mr. Rattenbury in his present state of gloom. He read passages with approval to his wife from time to time and repeated his admiration of anyone who could commit suicide in such circumstances. Mr. Rattenbury became more and more depressed.

Again Mrs. Rattenbury tried to cheer him up, and suggested a visit to Bridport for both of them on the next day. Mr. Rattenbury assented to this. His partner in the flat-building proposition lived there, and Mr. Rattenbury thought it might be possible to make some more favourable financial adjustment. Mrs. Rattenbury telephoned at once to Bridport and arranged for herself and her husband to stay the following night with their friend. The telephone was in Mr. Rattenbury's bedroom, which was next door to the drawing-room.

While Mrs. Rattenbury was still telephoning, Stoner came into the room. He was very angry and he had in his hand what Mrs. Rattenbury thought was a revolver but which proved to be a toy pistol. As this is the crucial point in the case, it will perhaps be better to give what followed in Mrs. Rattenbury's own words, from her examination-in-chief at the trial:

What did Stoner say he would do to you?—He said he would kill me if I went to Bridport.

Could you go on talking there without being overheard by your husband?—Yes, we could have done, because Mr. Rattenbury did not really take very much notice. We went into the dining-room to continue the conversation. Stoner still had the revolver. He accused me of living with Mr. Rattenbury that afternoon with the bedroom door closed.

What did you say to him?—I told him I had not. I told him not to make an ass of himself.

What did he then say?—He told me I must never have the bedroom door closed again, and that if I went to Bridport he would not drive. He was very annoyed at me going to Bridport. We had rather an unpleasant time about it. Afterwards I thought it was all right.

Did he give any reasons why you were not to go to Bridport?—He did not want me to be with Mr. Rattenbury. He was very jealous of Mr. Rattenbury—unnecessarily so. He thought I would have to share the same bedroom. I assured him I would have a separate bedroom.

What effect did that seem to have on him?—I thought it was all right, but I suppose he could not have taken it seriously. He could not have believed me.

MR. JUSTICE HUMPHREYS: But he seemed to have believed you and to be all right?—Yes.

This artless passage sheds a remarkable light on the relations in this strange household, with a middle-aged woman receiving orders, threats and reproaches from her young servant and the sexagenarian husband "not really taking very much notice" as he meditated on suicide in the adjoining room.

Mrs. Rattenbury was not asked anything about her own feelings regarding this almost demented jealousy of Stoner's, but it is not difficult to imagine that it was not altogether displeasing to her.

In any case she disregarded it, for she returned to the drawing-room and talked to her husband "about how nice it was that we were going to Bridport the next day. I tried to make him jolly."

Later Mrs. Rattenbury put John to bed, and then played cards with her husband in the drawing-room. "He seemed quite jolly then."

There was a little dog called Diana in the house, and it was Mrs. Rattenbury's practice to put her out into the garden each night through the French windows in the drawing-room, Mr. Rattenbury letting her in five minutes later. (This seems to show that Mr. Rattenbury, although "jolly" every night, was not helpless.) On this particular night she put the dog out as usual and closed the windows, after which she kissed Mr. Rattenbury good-night, saying: "Good night, darling." "I always kissed him good-night," she remarked in her evidence.

She went upstairs to the bathroom and then to her bedroom, where the little boy, too, was now asleep. In the bedroom she found the dog. Since the afternoon Mrs. Rattenbury had been wearing pyjamas, with her own underclothes underneath. She now undressed and resumed the pyjamas, did a little packing in preparation for the visit to Bridport, and got into bed. Expecting Stoner, she did not go to sleep but got out of bed from time to time as she thought of something else to put into her suit-case.

At a few minutes past ten Miss Riggs returned to the house. As she came in she saw Stoner hanging over the banisters, looking down into the hall. He told her that he was seeing if the lights were out. This seems to have given Miss Riggs an uneasy feeling, and hearing what she thought to be unusual breathing, she went to investigate. She switched on the light in Mr. Rattenbury's bedroom with the "premonition that something was wrong", but seeing that he was not in bed thought he might be asleep in his chair in the drawing-room and did not wish to disturb him there. Her premonition now allayed, Miss Riggs went upstairs.

Shortly after she had got into bed Mrs. Rattenbury came into her room and talked to her for ten minutes or so about the expedition to Bridport on the following day. Mrs. Rattenbury seemed a little excited over the trip in her usual way, but not unduly so, and apart from this there was noth-

ing abnormal in her manner. Having discussed the prepa-
rations with Miss Riggs, Mrs. Rattenbury returned to bed.

As to what happened next, in Mrs. Rattenbury's bedroom, we have only Mrs. Rattenbury's word for it; and in
view of the very different statements which Mrs. Rattenbury
herself made later, and which were of course given great
prominence in the press, there is every excuse for caution.
Nevertheless, Mrs. Rattenbury impressed everyone who
heard her at her trial as an exceptionally truthful witness,
telling the truth even when it was against herself, and the
version she then gave is probably the correct one. At any
rate it tallies with other evidence, and is perfectly reasonable.

According to Mrs. Rattenbury, then, Stoner came into
her bedroom shortly after she had returned from Miss Riggs.
He was in his pyjamas and got into bed with her. He seemed
agitated, and Mrs. Rattenbury asked him what the matter
was. Stoner replied that he was in trouble but could not tell
her what it was. On Mrs. Rattenbury insisting, Stoner said
that she would not be able to bear it. Mrs. Rattenbury,
thinking that the trouble had to do with some private affair
of Stoner's outside the household, answered that she was
strong enough to bear anything. Stoner then told her that
she was not going to Bridport the next day, because he had
hurt Mr. Rattenbury. He added that he had hit Mr. Rattenbury over the head with a mallet and hidden the mallet out
of doors.

At first Mrs. Rattenbury did not understand what Stoner
meant, until she heard Mr. Rattenbury groan in the room
below. It was, as she described it later, "a jolly good
groan". Hearing it, Mrs. Rattenbury jumped out of bed and
ran downstairs. Miss Riggs, in her own bedroom, heard her
go.

This is Mrs. Rattenbury's own description of what followed:

> I found Mr. Rattenbury sitting in that chair. I tried
> to rub his hands. They were cold. I tried to take his

pulse, and shook him to make him speak. I did not call
for help right away. I tried to make him speak first.
Then I saw this blood, and went around the table. I
trod on his false teeth. That made me hysterical and I
yelled. I took a drink of whisky to save myself being
sick, and yelled for Irene. I drank some whisky neat.
I tried to become senseless, to blot out the picture.

From that point Mrs. Rattenbury's memory afterwards
failed, perhaps conveniently. She remembered being sick
after her whisky, and putting a towel round her husband's
head, but nothing more. She did not remember even sending for the doctor.

Mrs. Rattenbury estimated that it was three minutes after
she got downstairs before she called for Miss Riggs. Miss
Riggs jumped up at once and hurried downstairs. She found
Mrs. Rattenbury in the drawing-room in her pyjamas, her
feet bare. Mr. Rattenbury was sitting in his armchair, unconscious, and Miss Riggs noticed that he had what appeared
to be a black eye. Mrs. Rattenbury was in a state of hysterical terror: a changed woman from the wildly excited con-
versationalist of ten minutes before. She was talking
incoherently to her husband, and Miss Riggs could distin-
guish no words but "Oh, poor 'Rats', what has happened?"
The scene Miss Riggs described later as "dreadful".

Seeing Miss Riggs, Mrs. Rattenbury told her to telephone
for the doctor. Miss Riggs did so, and Mrs. Rattenbury
added that Stoner was to hurry off in the car to see if the
doctor could be brought a little more quickly. Miss Riggs
therefore called Stoner down. Mrs. Rattenbury was still
somewhat hysterical, and kept calling out in agitated im-
patience: "Hurry, hurry! Can't somebody do something?"
Before going off in the car, Stoner helped the two women
carry Mr. Rattenbury into his adjoining bedroom and put
him on the bed.

The prosecution made a point at the trial that Mrs. Rattenbury called Miss Riggs downstairs and not Stoner, "the
man whom, in the circumstances, you might have supposed

she would have called if it were nothing more than a case of illness''. This, however, seems a point of doubtful value. The moment of confrontation with a corpse or near-corpse is of great importance in determining the amount of pre-knowledge on the part of a suspect. Mrs. Rattenbury seems to have acted in a perfectly natural way, as if she had suddenly received a great shock and not merely the minor shock of seeing in its actuality the grim scene she expected. And in the case of such a shock it was surely more natural for her to summon first the reliable friend of many years standing than the younger partner of her passions. It is a sign of the weakness of the subsequent case against Mrs. Rattenbury that it should have been felt necessary to emphasize such insignificant matters.

While waiting for the doctor Mrs. Rattenbury filled up the time by roaming the house and continuously drinking whisky-and-soda. At her instructions Miss Riggs cleared up most of the blood in the drawing-room; she also tried to wash Mr. Rattenbury's coat and waistcoat in the bathroom. Mrs. Rattenbury insisted on her doing this, because she did not wish the little boy to be upset by the sight of the blood the next morning. There was, in consequence, little blood about when the doctor arrived, and Miss Riggs' statement, therefore, becomes all the more important, that when she first reached the drawing-room she noticed that the blood lying around was not fresh but already thick and congealed. This, at any rate, shows that Mrs. Rattenbury could not have committed the murder herself just before Miss Riggs' arrival; and in view of the complete lack of material evidence concerning the actual commission of the crime, any fact which proves anything at all in this case is welcome.

When the doctor arrived he found the door of the house open, and walked in. Mrs. Rattenbury met him with wild excitement, still in her pyjamas, with bare feet, a glass of whisky in her hand, and the doctor thought that she was already a little intoxicated. She took him into the bedroom, where Mr. Rattenbury was lying partially dressed on the bed with a bloodstained towel round his head. The doctor noticed that Mr. Rattenbury's breathing was laboured, and asked what had happened. Mrs. Rattenbury replied: "Look at him! Look at the blood! Somebody has tried to finish him."

The doctor, seeing that the case was a surgical one, telephoned for Mr. 'Rooke, a Boscombe surgeon. While they were waiting for the latter's arrival Mrs. Rattenbury told the doctor how happy her husband had been at the prospect of the trip to Bridport on the following day, and how he had read to her a passage in a book about suicide. She tried to show the doctor the book, which was on the piano, but the doctor told her he had no time to bother with it. Mrs. Rattenbury also told the doctor that she had gone to bed and been aroused by a cry or a noise of some sort, had gone downstairs, and had found her husband in his chair with a pool of blood on the carpet.

It will be noticed that in this, the first of many statements she made, Mrs. Rattenbury is (a) shielding Stoner, (b) introducing the suicide suggestion, (c) leaving the way open to an assault by a stranger. At her trial the impression was, of course, conveyed that all this was done deliberately, in pursuance of a pre-arranged plan, and hysteria is not at this point admitted. That is only recognized when Mrs. Rattenbury goes on later to accuse herself, the suggestion being that she then, in hysterical frenzy, threw away all her carefully-planned defences and screamed out the truth.

To understand the real situation is, however, not difficult. Assuming that Mrs. Rattenbury's version of what happened upstairs is correct, she knew from the beginning that it was Stoner who had done this to her husband. That her husband should have been attacked by a stranger would, of course, have provoked a *crise des nerfs* in this highly-strung woman; but it would not, I think, have produced such extreme reactions as Mrs. Rattenbury did, in fact, display. It was the knowledge that Stoner's hand was responsible for the attack that upset her even more than the attack itself. This particularly accounts for her efforts to drug her mind with whisky. It was not as she said the "picture" that she wished to "blot out'' but the instinctively unwelcome knowledge of the artist's identity.

To shield Stoner was therefore her first aim, conscious or unconscious; and to do this she was ready to throw out any suggestion, however absurd, that jumped into her mind. This, combined with alcohol, is the only way to account for so preposterous a theory as that Mr. Rattenbury committed suicide by striking himself repeatedly on the head with a mallet. (In the early newspaper accounts of this case, prominence was given to an alleged statement of Mrs. Rattenbury's: "He did it himself. He did it with a mallet." This statement, if it was ever made at all, was not adduced in evidence at the trial.)

When Mr. Rooke arrived he was able to make only a cursory examination of Mr. Rattenbury; he found it impossible to make a thorough one both on account of the blood and of the disturbance to which he was subjected. Mrs. Rattenbury was pressing her attentions on her husband to such an extent as to impede the surgeon in his work; she was trying to remove his shirt and calling for scissors with which to do so, and making remarks which appeared to Mr. Rooke incoherent. He tried to persuade her to keep away from the bed without success, and seeing that she was in an abnormal state Mr. Rooke considered that the only thing was to have Mr. Rattenbury removed to a nursing-home.

This was accordingly done, and on a further examination there it was found that the bone on the left side of Mr. Rattenbury's head had been driven into the brain. Three blows appeared to have been dealt him. The first, in Mr. Rooke's opinion, was a blow above the ear, delivered probably from behind. This would have the effect of making Mr. Rattenbury crumple up in a forward direction. Two further blows were then struck as he was toppling over.

When the doctors had made these discoveries, it became plain that the question of accident could be dismissed and that Mr. Rattenbury was suffering from applied violence. In consequence, the doctor, who had hitherto been considering the possibility that Mr. Rattenbury might have had a fall and hit his head against a piece of furniture, telephoned his information to the police.

From this point the sequence of events, as it was disjointedly presented in court, becomes somewhat confused; but disentangling the story as best one may, I think the following account is tolerably accurate.

The first policeman to arrive at the Villa Madeira was P.C. Bagwell. To him Mrs. Rattenbury, now thoroughly drunk, said:

> I was playing cards with my husband until nine o'clock. Then I went to my bedroom. At about 10.30 I heard a yell and came downstairs into the drawing-room. I saw my husband sitting in the armchair and sent for Dr. O'Donnell.

This is a fairly coherent statement, for "the accused then said". It must, however, be remembered, both in regard to this and still more to later statements of Mrs. Rattenbury's as reported officially, that these police versions of remarks made by suspected persons are often extremely misleading on three counts. In the first place, the context of circumstances is omitted, and these are in the highest degree important; in the second, only the words used by the suspect are written down, and not anything said by the policeman; thirdly, intervals of time are not noted, so that remarks are often made to appear consecutive, which were, in fact, not so. One must therefore remember the conditions at the Villa Madeira at this time, with Mrs. Rattenbury tolerably drunk and half the time incoherent in her speech, playing the radio-gramophone, and, no doubt, screaming disjointed replies to the policeman's questions, interrupting Miss Riggs and with Miss Riggs interrupting her, while the policeman wrote down in his note-book what he saw and what he heard, perhaps even being shaken and jogged by Mrs. Rattenbury while he was doing so.

P.C. Bagwell was followed by Inspector Mills. It was now past midnight, and the atmosphere in the little drawing-

room instead of growing calmer was becoming still more
hectic. To the Inspector Mrs. Rattenbury explained how, on
hearing groans, she had come downstairs and found her
husband in the chair with the blood flowing from his head.
In answer to a question of the Inspector's, she also told him
that the French windows, which at this time were open, had
been shut and locked when she first came downstairs. Inspector Mills, of course, realized that this meant that no
one could have come in from outside, struck the blows, and
escaped the same way; in other words, the assailant must
probably be some member of the household.

Inspector Mills then went off to have a look round, and
Mrs. Rattenbury was left alone with P.C. Bagwell, to whom
she is alleged to have made the following "statement":

> I know who did it. [Here the constable cautioned
> her.] I did it with a mallet. It is hidden. Rats has lived
> too long. No, my lover did it. I will give you £10. No,
> I won't bribe you.

This is obviously no statement, but a series of discon-
nected remarks, some of them no doubt made in reply to
questions. However, the importance of these wild words is
that the mallet is now mentioned for the first time, and for
the first time Mrs. Rattenbury is accusing herself.

What followed after this is not quite clear; but in spite
of Mrs. Rattenbury's incriminating words, both the policemen seem to have withdrawn from the house, Inspector
Mills to go to the nursing-home for a word with the doctors, and P.C. Bagwell for another and more modest reason. For Mrs. Rattenbury, it seems, was now pressing her
attentions upon him to an embarrassing degree. She was,
in fact, trying to kiss him; and the constable was not willing to be kissed. He therefore withdrew, telling Miss Riggs
that he was going to fetch another police-officer, presumably to protect him.

Mrs. Rattenbury and Miss Riggs were now left alone in

the house. Stoner was still waiting in the car outside the nursing-home, where Inspector Mills saw him, apparently peacefully asleep.

All this time Mrs. Rattenbury had been drinking at intervals, and according to her own account she was not used to whisky. In any case she was now very drunk indeed; so drunk that she took it very hard to be deprived of her policeman. She tried to get out of the house after him, rushing from one door to another. Miss Riggs had, however, locked them all and taken out the keys. This extraordinary tragifarce receives its final touch in an answer made by Miss Riggs in her evidence at the trial. When asked how she managed to detain Mrs. Rattenbury in the house during this period and keep her from pursuit of the fleeing policeman, Miss Riggs replied simply: "I was sitting on her in the dining-room."

Inspector Mills also seems to have been a little apprehensive of this wild woman. "I have been to Manor Road," he told the doctor, at the nursing-home, "but that woman is drunk."

Later, P.C. Bagwell arrived with his bodyguard, all of whom at once began to ask Mrs. Rattenbury questions. Presumably, however, they did not get much out of her, for, according to Miss Riggs, "at times you could make out what she was saying, but at others you could not".

Inspector Mills returned to the villa at about 3.30 a.m. He told Mrs. Rattenbury that her husband's condition was a critical one, and she replied: "Will this be against me?" The Inspector cautioned her, and Mrs. Rattenbury then made another "statement":

> I did it. He gave me the book. He has lived too long. He said, "Dear, dear." I will tell you in the morning where the mallet is. Have you told the coroner yet? I shall make a better job of it next time. Irene does not know. I made a proper muddle of it. I thought I was strong enough.

Fortunately, we have a picture of the conditions under which this "statement" was made, for the doctor arrived back from the nursing-home at about this time, driven by Stoner, and this is his description of the scene that met him:

> I found Mrs. Rattenbury intoxicated and excited. The radio-gramophone was playing and there were four police officers in the house, and she was running about among them from room to room. I tried to explain to her her husband's condition, but she could not take it in. I thought the only thing to do was to stop the exhibition I saw by giving her morphia.

As soon as she saw him Mrs. Rattenbury rushed towards the doctor, who took her upstairs and administered to her the large but justifiable dose of half a grain of morphia hypodermically in the arm. Mrs. Rattenbury, however, was not to be quietened so easily. Before the morphia could take effect she was downstairs again making another wild "statement".

In this instance we have two witnesses to what was said, and a comparison of their evidence is not uninstructive. According to Inspector Mills:

> Mrs. Rattenbury came downstairs and said, "I know who did it—his son." I asked her how old the son was, and she replied, "Thirty-two, but he is not here." Dr. O'Donnell came into the room and said, "I have given her morphia. I don't think she is fit to make a statement."

And according to the doctor:

> I went downstairs and saw Miss Riggs and Stoner to see if I could find out anything. When I returned to the sitting-room about five minutes later I found Mrs. Rattenbury was there. Inspector Mills was in the room, and he asked her, "Do you suspect anybody?" Her reply was, "Yes." "Whom do you suspect?" the offi-

cer asked, and she said, "I think his son did it." Inspector Mills asked Mrs. Rattenbury, "What age is his son?" Her reply was, "Thirty-six." The Inspector asked, "Where is his son?" and she said, "I don't know." I asked Inspector Mills if he had cautioned the lady, and his reply was "No." I then said, "Look at her condition. She is full of whisky and I have just given her a large dose of morphia. She is not fit to make a statement to you or anybody else."

It will be noticed that the Inspector's version, while not exactly inaccurate, is nevertheless somewhat selective as well as condensed. The doctor's is not only more vivid, but conveys far more correctly what really occurred. The apparent and silly non-sequitur "thirty-two, but he is not here", from the Inspector's note-book, is typical, as is the implication that Mrs. Rattenbury volunteered the first sentence of this "statement". From the doctor's evidence we see that the latter was not made on the speaker's own initiative but was in reply to a question, and there was no non-sequitur at all.

After this Mrs. Rattenbury really was got to bed, though not without difficulty, and the doctor, having supervised this operation, left the house. It must by now have been after 4 a.m.

During nearly all this time, ever since he had been sent to bring the doctor, Stoner had been outside the house. He had no idea that Mrs. Rattenbury had been making "statements", and he had had no chance of consulting with her, nor indeed did he appear to want one. After Mrs. Rattenbury had gone to bed, Stoner appears to have "walked about the house", but no one enlightened him as to anything Mrs. Rattenbury had said. Inspector Mills asked him once if he had seen a mallet anywhere, and Stoner replied that he had not; if he wondered how the Inspector could know anything about a mallet, he kept his curiosity to himself.

In spite of the morphia Mrs. Rattenbury was not to be allowed much sleep. Not in bed till four o'clock or there-

abouts, she was being badgered again shortly after six. At
that time Detective-Inspector Carter, a recent arrival on the
scene, and Miss Riggs went up to her bedroom, taking coffee with them with which to pull Mrs. Rattenbury together.
They seem to have got some of the coffee down her, but
according to Miss Riggs Mrs. Rattenbury was unable to
hold the cup and could drink only ''after a fashion''. She
was, however, sufficiently roused to cause this entry in the
Detective-Inspector's note-book, dated 6.10 a.m.:

> I picked up the mallet and he dared me to hit him.
> He said, ''You have not guts enough to do it.'' I hit
> him and hid the mallet. He is not dead, is he? Are you
> the coroner?

The officer decided, however, that Mrs. Rattenbury was
''not normal'', and these remarks of hers were in consequence not put in as evidence at the trial. Not, however,
that anything was lost by the omission, for Mrs. Rattenbury's next ''statement'' repeated them word for word, with
the omission only of the last question.

Mrs. Rattenbury may not have been normal at this early
hour, nevertheless she was ordered, or persuaded, or per-
mitted out of bed a few minutes later, and sent to have a
bath. According to Detective-Inspector Carter she was anxious to get up, and for a time he would not allow her to do
so; according to counsel for the defence, the Detective-
Inspector insisted on feeding her coffee and sending her to
have a bath in order to create the semblance of her being in
a reasonable condition for the taking of a statement. The
onlooker must choose which version is more likely to be
the correct one; though it is possible to say that even a
person as highly strung as Mrs. Rattenbury would have difficulty in throwing off the effects of a half-grain of morphia
after barely two hours' sleep.

After her bath Mrs. Rattenbury seems to have held a kind
of police-reception in her bedroom, willy or nilly. In any
case, Miss Riggs is reported to have said something to this

effect: "Give the woman a chance; she can't get dressed with three police-officers in the room." To this plea, however, Detective-Inspector Carter must have turned a literally deaf ear, for he could not afterwards remember ever having heard it. However, when a police-matron arrived the officers left the room. That an official eye had at this stage to be kept on Mrs. Rattenbury is, of course, undeniable; but three pairs of official eyes was, perhaps, overdoing it. Possibly, however, the distressing experience of P.C. Bagwell was still in the minds of these officers, and they were clinging together by way of mutual protection.

During the small hours, investigations by the police had not been unfruitful, and in the garden there had been found a mallet to which human hairs and a piece of skin were still adhering.

While waiting for Mrs. Rattenbury to get dressed, under the supervision of the police-matron, Detective-Inspector Carter took the following statement from Stoner at 7.30 a.m.:

I retired to my bedroom at about 8.5 p.m. on Sunday, March 24th, leaving Mr. and Mrs. Rattenbury and the boy John in the drawing-room. About 10.30 I was aroused by Mrs. Rattenbury shouting to me to come down. I came down into the drawing-room and saw Mr. Rattenbury sitting in the armchair with blood running from his head. Mrs. Rattenbury was crying and screaming and said to me, "Help me to get 'Rats' to bed. He has been hurt." I then took the car and went to Dr. O'Donnell's house. He had left before I got there. When I returned, on the instructions of Mrs. Rattenbury I cleaned the blood from the floor. Mrs. Rattenbury was sober, and as far as I know she had not been drinking. When I went to bed she was in a normal condition.

I have never seen a mallet on the premises. Until I was aroused I heard no sound of a quarrel or any noise of any kind. Since September 1934 I have been em-

ployed by Mr. and Mrs. Rattenbury. They have been
on the best of terms. I said to her, "How did this
happen?" She said, "I do not know." Mr. Rattenbury
was fully dressed in the armchair and Mrs. Rattenbury
was dressed in pyjamas and had bare feet.

This "statement" bears unmistakable signs of having been
obtained by question and answer, and the prompting behind it
shows clearly through. There is, of course, no objection at all
to a police-officer obtaining information this way and then
summarizing it. The objection is to calling the result a "statement". It is not. The term "statement" should be limited to
a spontaneous production on the part of the stater, in his own
words and without promptings or suggestions. To call a mere
summary of interrogation a "statement" is to destroy the importance of the genuine article.

It will be noticed from this "statement" that Stoner seems,
at this stage, to have no story ready to account for the attack
on Mr. Rattenbury. Had he had one in his mind, he would
surely have put it forward during this interrogation. It is, of
course, possible that he did so, and that Detective-Inspector
Carter, having already made up his mind that Mrs. Rattenbury was the guilty person (and, indeed, at this point with
every justification), did not think it worth including in the
summary; and if this is the case, it is a pity. There is no
reason at all for assuming that this is what happened, though
we do know that police-officers are occasionally inclined to
be a little too selective as to what they include in these
summaries. The point is, however, not a negligible one,
and it would be interesting to have this possible doubt
cleared up. The degree of premeditation in Mr. Rattenbury's murder is difficult to assess, and any fact which has
some bearing on this question deserves scrutiny. In the same
way, any evidence as to Stoner's intelligence, or lack of it,
is important. If, nine hours after the crime, Stoner had not
produced some story to explain Mr. Rattenbury's death
without incriminating either himself or Mrs. Rattenbury,
this is a large point against premeditation as well as a tol-

erable proof of stupidity. (Or, if premeditation had nevertheless existed, the proof is that of an almost incredible
degree of stupidity.) If, on the other hand, some such story
was hinted at, even if not developed, it would be extremely
interesting to know what it was. Lastly, if Stoner suggested
no theory, not so much through inability to invent one as
on account of mental inertia, and was merely standing by
in masterly inactivity, waiting to see what might develop
and under the impression that there was no incriminating
evidence against either himself or Mrs. Rattenbury (and this
is perhaps the most likely explanation), then he was an exceedingly stupid young man. And I think Stoner must have
been an exceedingly stupid young man.

At 8.15 Mrs. Rattenbury was dressed and ready, and
Detective-Inspector Carter again attended her in her bedroom. To him she now appeared to be perfectly normal and
no longer under the influence of drugs. From other evidence, however, it appears that with the Detective-Inspector
the wish was father to the self-deception. At the trial Mrs.
Rattenbury's counsel naturally suggested that it was unfair
to question her in this state. But was it? The Detective-
Inspector had every reason, at this stage, to believe that it
was she who had made the attack on her husband, and he
wanted the truth. It may well have seemed to him that he
had a better chance of getting it, in the case of a woman of
Mrs. Rattenbury's temperament, when she had not too many
of her rather volatile wits about her. If that was his hope, it
was not to be fulfilled.

In any case, at 8.15 Detective-Inspector Carter first cautioned her and then charged her with doing grievous bodily
harm with intent to murder. (At this time, of course, Mr.
Rattenbury was still alive.) Mrs. Rattenbury thereupon made
a "statement", which of all the 'statements' connected with
this case looks most like a genuine one:

About 9 p.m. on March 24 I was playing cards with
my husband when he dared me to kill him, as he
wanted to die. I picked up a mallet and he then said,

"You have not guts enough to do it." I then hit him
with the mallet. I hid the mallet outside the house. I
would have shot him if I had had a gun.

According to Detective-Inspector Carter, Mrs. Rattenbury appeared to understand what she was saying and doing, and before signing the statement she read it aloud quite
clearly.

Mrs. Rattenbury was then escorted out of the house. In
the hall were Stoner and Miss Riggs. Mrs. Rattenbury said
to them: "Don't make fools of yourselves." Stoner replied:
"You have got yourself into this mess by talking too much."
This remark seems to have a touch of asperity, and no doubt
Stoner felt that he had reason for annoyance.

After this somewhat dramatic encounter Mrs. Rattenbury
was taken to Bournemouth Police Station, where she was
charged. In reply she said: "That's right. I did it deliberately, and I would do it again."

What was Stoner doing, to allow his mistress to be
arrested like this under his very nose? What was
Mrs. Rattenbury doing, confessing to the murder in this
exceedingly unnatural and almost studiedly callous way?

As to the first question, counsel for the prosecution answered it in his own way. He suggested that the two sen-
tences exchanged in the hall between Mrs. Rattenbury and
Stoner, combined with Stoner's willingness to see Mrs. Rattenbury arrested, indicated a conspiracy to murder between
the two of them; for in that case it would be merely bad
luck should one be taken, with no moral obligation on the
other to come forward too. This is a perfectly sound argument, and the words used in the hall are quite capable of
bearing this construction. On the other hand, there is an
equally good argument against conspiracy even at this stage,
and that is the absence of any common story between the
two. Surely if they had planned the murder between them,
almost one of the first things they would decide would be
the story they were to tell the police. Even if Stoner was
stupid enough to omit this, Mrs. Rattenbury certainly was

not. (Curiously, Mrs. Rattenbury's counsel does not seem
to have used exactly this argument. His point against conspiracy was the absence from Mrs. Rattenbury's first two
statements of any alibis, mutual or otherwise, for herself
and, presumably, Stoner.)

Perhaps it is not difficult to realize why Stoner stood by
and watched Mrs. Rattenbury being carried off. We must
put ourselves in his place. He was very young, and Mrs.
Rattenbury must always have seemed to him the person on
whom to rely—which is not by any means the same thing
as believing that he was as much under her domination as
all sides at the trial seemed to agree. He must have been
expecting her to get him somehow out of the mess. Perhaps
he did not believe that she could be in any serious danger.
He had not heard her charged. And to speak just then was
so very final. It could do no harm to wait. And mingled
with all this there was probably that curious annoyance
which we sometimes feel when someone of whom we are
fond is hurt or made unhappy: a selfish annoyance, coming
from resentment that our own feelings should be lacerated,
too, on account of our very fondness. A tinge of that might
well have decided Stoner, dithering as he must have been,
whether to speak or not.

As for Mrs. Rattenbury, she had no such hesitations. She
had confessed, without any word as to a conspiracy, in order
to save Stoner. There can be no other possible reason, except that she was speaking the truth; and she is entitled to
full credit for what she did, because she certainly was not
speaking the truth. It may well be, however, that she felt a
big share of responsibility for what had happened to her
husband, without which she would hardly have undertaken
the full consequences. In any case, and even discounting
the hazy hang-over from the morphia, Mrs. Rattenbury did
a plucky thing, entirely in accordance with the public-school
code.

With regard to this hang-over it is worth noting that, when
her own doctor saw Mrs. Rattenbury at the police-station,
he found her still so much under the influence of the mor-

phia that she appeared dazed and was swaying and unable to walk without support. The prison doctor also found the effects persisting for another two days. Besides invalidating the statements she made on the morning of March 25th, this also conclusively shows that Mrs. Rattenbury could not have been a drug-fiend as well as a drinker, as the prosecution rather unnecessarily suggested later.

Just before the police-officer took her away from the house Mrs. Rattenbury whispered to Miss Riggs: "Tell Stoner he must give me the mallet." The significance of this is obvious. Miss Riggs duly passed on the message, but Stoner did not have a chance to answer because Miss Riggs herself added: "But I see the police have got it."

Mrs. Rattenbury now passes out of the picture, and we have a curious situation at the Villa Madeira, where Miss Riggs now knows perfectly well who killed Mr. Rattenbury, but apparently does nothing about it, and Stoner knows she knows. Stoner indeed went so far as to say to Miss Riggs, soon after Mrs. Rattenbury had been taken away: "I suppose you know who did it." According to Miss Riggs herself, she made no reply to this, and nothing further was said. Presumably, however, the two eyed each other at intervals in what used to be known as an old-fashioned way.

In this remarkable state of neutrality Miss Riggs and Stoner seem to have lived at the Villa Madeira for three days, with an occasional exchange to keep up the tension. On one occasion, for instance, Miss Riggs asked Stoner if there would be his fingerprints on the mallet, to which Stoner replied with complete frankness: "No, I wore gloves." If this is correctly reported, it is by far the most important statement that Stoner made.

Then, on the Tuesday, Miss Riggs asked Stoner, almost casually, why he had done it. Stoner answered because he had seen Mr. Rattenbury with Mrs. Rattenbury in the afternoon. (When Miss Riggs testified to this reply, the judge asked her, not without reason, whether Stoner was sober when he made it. Miss Riggs affirmed that he was perfectly sober. The mystery must therefore remain.)

On this day, too, Miss Riggs drove with Stoner to Wimborne, for some reason unnamed, and on the way back Stoner pointed to a house where an ex-policeman lived, and said that the occupant could bear him out that he was out that way at about 8.30 on the Sunday evening. This remark, brought out in Miss Riggs' examination-in-chief, was not followed up at the trial, and its significance is not apparent, except that it contradicts Stoner's first statement to Detective-Inspector Carter that he went up to his bedroom that evening at 8.15.

On the Wednesday evening Stoner was a little drunk, and appeared upset too. He called to Miss Riggs to come to him in his bedroom, as he wanted to speak to her "on her own." Upon Miss Riggs complying, Stoner confided to her that Mrs. Rattenbury was in gaol and it was he who had put her there; and he was going up to see her and give himself up. No doubt Miss Riggs approved of this course for reasons of her own as well as for the sake of justice; for Stoner's admissions during these days had put her, strictly speaking, in the position of an accessory after the fact. Miss Riggs must have appreciated this, for in the end she gave the police the information which it was her duty to pass on to them.

On this day Mrs. Rattenbury wrote to Stoner from prison:

I must see you, darling. Please write to me. This is the third letter I have written. Hope you receive this. I hardly know how to write now. Let me know how 'Rats' is getting on. No more now. God bless you. My love be with you always.

LOZANNE

Have you talked with Dr. O'D. about how 'Rats' is? Goodness, there is so much I want to know! Please ask Irene to give you a few bobbing pins for my hair. I think they will be allowed.

On Thursday morning Miss Riggs woke at 6.30 and heard
Stoner already getting up. He left the house at 6.50, came
back about ten minutes later, and then left again. Later in
the day—where, when, or in what circumstances we are not
told—he was arrested by Detective-Inspector Carter and
taken to Bournemouth Police Station. When charged, he
replied, "I understand." There is no information as to
whether Stoner's arrest was unexpected by himself or
whether he gave himself up; but if the former, we may at
any rate give him credit for the right intention. Stoner may
not have been a pleasing character, but he had at any rate
this elementary decency once he realized that Mrs. Rattenbury's position really was a serious one.

On this day Mr. Rattenbury died, at the nursing-home,
without having recovered consciousness. It was therefore
with his murder that Stoner was charged.

The next day, in the detention-room of the Bournemouth
police-court, Stoner remarked to the constable on duty: "Do
you know Mrs. Rattenbury had nothing to do with this affair?"

The constable cautioned him, but Stoner went on:

> When I did the job I believe he was asleep. I hit him
> and then went upstairs and told Mrs. Rattenbury. She
> rushed down then. You see, I watched through the
> french window and saw her kiss him good night—then
> leave the room. I waited, and then crept in through the
> french window, which was unlocked. I think he must
> have been asleep when I hit him. Still, it ain't much
> use saying anything. I don't suppose they will let her
> out yet. You know, there should be a doctor with her
> when they tell her I'm arrested, because she will go
> out of her mind.

This statement seems spontaneous, and its interest needs
no underlining. In view of what was suggested later, however, it is worth noting here that this statement is important
not only for what it includes but for what it omits. There

is, for instance, no hint that Stoner had been inhaling cocaine on the Sunday evening.

Mrs. Rattenbury had appeared first before the magistrates on March 25th, and been remanded. When she appeared again, with Stoner, on April 3rd, she was charged with murder, jointly with Stoner. The case opened on April 11th, and continued from week to week in the usual way.

In the meantime the inquest on Mr. Rattenbury had been opened on April 2nd, for formal evidence of death only. The police surgeon gave evidence that the cause of death was laceration of and haemorrhage into the brain and into the skull, as a result of a compound fracture produced by injuries. The coroner pressed him to add that the injury was produced by a blow, but the surgeon very properly refused. The inquest was then adjourned till June 27th. By that date the trial was over, and a non-committal verdict was returned to the effect that the damage as detailed by the police surgeon had been produced by "a violent injury".

On April 18th Mrs. Rattenbury wrote a letter to Miss Riggs containing the following passages:

Oh, Lord! To-morrow Good Friday and I dare not think of the children. I have been pretending I have not any here. If one thought for five minutes they would go mad. Good Friday will be like Sunday here. Of all the days in the week, Sunday is the worst.

I have to control my mind like the devil not to think of little John. Yes, take him out on Sundays, darling. C. was awfully pleased to hear from you. My M. not doing anything. Can you? Messages of love are not much use to me now, I want your help. . . . However, I feel awfully sad being separated in such a ghastly way from everything that one loves. S.'s feelings must take some weighing up, but he will be the same and not allow himself to think.

Should think his remorse at what he has brought upon my head, the children, etc.—smashed life—would drive him a raving lunatic. Frightful responsibility to

hold in one person's hands. God deliver me from such
a hellish responsibility. I cannot have courage enough
to bear that pain. My own is more than enough in a
hundred lifetimes as it is.

At times have found my feelings very hard and bit-
ter. Oh, my God, appallingly so, but have managed to
drown these feelings and get one's heart soft again.
Darling, God bless you; bless us all and get us out of
this nightmare. My love to your M. and F. My love be
with you always.

LOZANNE

Those interested in human problems may speculate why
Mrs. Rattenbury should have signed this letter to Miss Riggs
"Lozanne", a name which had never been used between
them before.

The magistrates having duly committed both Mrs. Rattenbury and Stoner, and the grand jury having returned a
true bill, their joint trial began at the Old Bailey on Monday,
May 27th, only just over two months from the date of the
murder. Queues waited hours for the opening of the court,
and unemployed men offered to sell their places for large
sums.

Mr. Justice Humphreys was on the bench, and Mr. R. P.
Croom-Johnson, K.C., M.P., led for the prosecution, as-
sisted by Mr. Anthony Hawke. For Mrs. Rattenbury were
Mr. T. J. O'Connor, K.C., and the Hon. E. E. Montague.
Mr. J. D. Casswell, fresh from a successful appeal for murder before the House of Lords, appeared for Stoner. Both
prisoners are reported as pleading not guilty in "faint but
firm voices".

While the jury were being sworn Mr. Casswell made an
application that the accused should be tried separately, and
on the direction of the judge the jury left the box while the
case was argued. Mr. Caswell quoted the letter written by
Mrs. Rattenbury to Miss Riggs on April 18th and submitted
that it showed a distinct intention to throw responsibility on
the other prisoner. Mr. Justice Humphreys held that there

was no ground for directing that there should be separate trials. Mr. Croom-Johnson accordingly opened the case for the prosecution.

He outlined the relations between Mrs. Rattenbury and Stoner, gave a short account of the events which took place on the night of March 24th, and produced the fatal mallet, suggesting that this was the "heavy instrument" which had made the three wounds on Mr. Rattenbury's head: which, in view of the human hairs and skin found upon it, it undoubtedly was. Mr. Croom-Johnson also quoted the various "statements" made by the accused and, concerning that made by Mrs. Rattenbury to Inspector Mills at 3.30 a.m., counsel commented:

> In the submission of the prosecution, if those words are right, blows were struck, according to this statement, by Mrs. Rattenbury, and the reason why they had not killed Mr. Rattenbury outright was that her physical strength was not sufficient.

It is a sign of the fairness with which Mr. Croom-Johnson conducted the prosecution, both in this speech and subsequently, that he should have qualified the submission of the prosecution so pointedly. It may also be a sign of Mr. Croom-Johnson's own opinion of the case which he had to present against the female prisoner.

Evidence was then called to prove the possession of the mallet by Stoner on the evening of March 24th. This mallet belonged to Stoner's uncle, and Stoner had borrowed it from his grandparents' house in the early evening of March 24th. He said that he wanted to drive in some tent-pegs with it. (In the reports of the trial as published in the daily press, no question is recorded to elucidate whether or not any tent-pegs were to be driven in during the next day or two at the Villa Madeira, so that one cannot judge whether this was a genuine reason for borrowing the mallet or an excuse. If no such question was ever put, this would seem a curious omission on the part of the prosecution, for the importance of this point is obvious so far as the degree of premeditation is concerned.)

The first important witness was Miss Irene Riggs, whose evidence occupied all the rest of the day. It included, however, nothing of importance which has not already been stated in this narrative. Miss Riggs was in the box five hours, and everyone, including the judge, was kind to her. In reply to Mr. Justice Humphreys Miss Riggs said that she had never known Mrs. Rattenbury take drugs, such as cocaine, morphia, or heroin.

Mrs. Rattenbury and Stoner had listened to the hearing intently but with expressionless faces. They sat at opposite ends of the dock, and took no notice of each other, not even by a glance. Mrs. Rattenbury kept her eyes fixed most of the time on the judge. Stoner, a little pale, appeared almost indifferent. Mrs. Rattenbury was wearing blue.

At midnight the queue began to form for the next day's hearing.

Police and medical evidence occupied the second day. A hare had been started to the effect that Mrs. Rattenbury drugged, in consequence of the finding of the hypodermic syringe and needles in the bathroom cupboard, and some time was wasted in chasing it before the explanation was reached that the syringe had been used for injections into Mrs. Rattenbury's elder son two years earlier. It was therefore finally accepted that Mrs. Rattenbury did not drug.

Cross-examination by the defence showed that Mrs. Rattenbury's own doctor was definitely sympathetic. He had no exalted opinion of Mrs. Rattenbury, but succeeded in making it plain between the words that he did not consider her capable of committing or planning this very crude murder. Discussing Mrs. Rattenbury's peculiar temperament with the witness, Mr. O'Connor put one telling question which the judge disallowed on the grounds that it was a matter for the jury to decide. Mr. O'Connor had, however, made his point:

As her medical attendant, and one who had every opportunity for seeing her temperament at close quarters, do you think it would be possible for Mrs. Rattenbury to take part in a crime of this description and then act perfectly normally and peacefully with her maid?

The witness's negative reply must have sounded almost as emphatically as if he had actually made it.

In his cross-examination for Stoner Mr. Casswell put his foot well down on the cocaine pedal and kept it there till he had forced the witness to admit that he had believed Stoner to be taking cocaine; the inference, which Mr. Casswell was too wily to press, being that the doctor still believed that Stoner had been taking cocaine. Another point which Mr. Casswell brought out was that when driving the doctor back from the nursing-home on the night of March 24th, Stoner had not appeared at all agitated or apprehensive.

The surgeon who had made the post-mortem testified that the three blows must have been dealt with very considerable force.

Mr. O'Connor made another cunning point for Mrs. Rattenbury in his cross-examination of Inspector Mills:

Did you follow up her statement, "I will tell you in the morning where the mallet is"?—No, I did not question her.

Was not that because you did not think she was in a fit condition to give intelligent answers?—No.

Why not ask her where the mallet was?—I did not ask her.

MR. JUSTICE HUMPHREYS (*to* MR. O'CONNOR): Do you really suggest that in these circumstances the police-officer should have cross-examined her?

MR. O'CONNOR: I do not suggest that. I do not blame him for not having pursued the point.

The judge, of course, knew perfectly well what Mr. O'Connor was really suggesting: that if Mrs. Rattenbury,

having shown willingness to hand over the mallet, had at
that point been pressed to do so, she would have been unable, because she did not know where it was—*ergo* it was
not she who had hidden it, *ergo* it was not she who had
used it. One cannot, of course, blame the Inspector for not
having pressed this inquiry when Mrs. Rattenbury was in
such a condition; nevertheless it is a pity that, fairly or
unfairly, he did not do so. The result would at least have
been interesting. It might even have settled definitely the
question of Mrs. Rattenbury's complicity, for or against.

On the third day it was first the turn of the experts.

Dr. Roche Lynch gave the weight of the mallet as 2 lb.
7 oz., and stated a cautious opinion that the hairs on it "in
all probability" came from the head of the deceased. In
cross-examination, Mr. Casswell tried hard to persuade him
to admit that a person who had shown such characteristics
as Stoner had, together with such symptoms as counsel was
apparently inferring Stoner had felt, though no very satisfactory evidence was ever called to prove them, must be a
cocaine addict. Mr. Casswell put his questions in such a
way that Dr. Roche Lynch could not help replying to many
of them in the affirmative; but Mr. Croom-Johnson destroyed, in re-examination, much more than Mr. Casswell
had gained, by two or three simple questions, eliciting the
facts that anyone who had taken two eggspoonfuls of cocaine would, even if a mild addict, become desperately ill
and would certainly not be able to drive a car within a few
hours.

It seems to have been in Brixton Prison, whither he was
transferred from Dorchester on May 14th, that Stoner began
to develop this drug-fiend defence; possibly as a result of a
certain successful interview which he had had at Dorchester. The senior medical officer of the former prison, Dr.
Grierson, deposed that Stoner had told him that he used to
take cocaine between slices of bread, and that at about 4.30
p.m. on March 24th he had scoffed two eggspoonfuls of it.
If so, he must have been almost more than habituated; yet
on May 14th he was rational in behaviour and conversation,

and since then had eaten and slept normally and gained 8 lb. in weight. Mr. Casswell, with his usual ingenuity, got round all these difficulties by suggesting that the interval at Dorchester Prison had been enough to wean Stoner from his craving and restore him to physical normality, and that cocaine is usually sold illegally in a much diluted form, so that it would be quite possible to take as much as two egg-spoonfuls of a sufficiently diluted mixture. With this evident fact Dr. Grierson had to agree. Once more, however, Mr. Croom-Johnson spiked his opponent's gun. Eliciting from the witness that Stoner had confided to him that cocaine always made him excited, causing him to curse and swear, Mr. Croom-Johnson asked simply: "Is that the usual effect of taking cocaine?" The witness replied that it was not; the usual effect of cocaine was to make people feel happy and contented. But the most fortunate item for Mr. Casswell in this witness's evidence was the fact that Stoner had described cocaine to Dr. Grierson as "a brown powder with black spots in it." There was no way of getting round this howler.

The medical officer of Dorchester Prison then deposed that during the time Stoner was under his care he showed none of the usual signs of a cocaine addict deprived of his drug; he seemed perfectly healthy and normal. Mr. Casswell prudently did not cross-examine this witness.

The case for the prosecution ended with witnesses to the stay of Mrs. Rattenbury and Stoner in London on March 19th and the purchases made for Stoner. Mr. O'Connor then at once called Mrs. Rattenbury.

For the third day in succession no recognition had passed between the prisoners. Mrs. Rattenbury now seemed tired, though she declined an offer of a chair in the witness-box, and a doctor was with her in the dock all day, as well as a wardress. Her evidence lasted three hours; and for those to whom a precedent may be welcome, it may be added that she wore "a smart blue dress and fur cape, with elbow-length blue gloves".

As has been said, Mrs. Rattenbury made a very favourable impression in the witness-box. She answered naturally, often using gesture to help out her meaning, and with composure; only when she was telling how she went downstairs and found her husband injured did she show emotion. She answered unpleasant questions with great frankness, and all those who heard her believed that what she said in the witness-box could really be relied on as the truth.

Nor did she try to gloss over or excuse her own conduct, as most witnesses do. In this connexion one passage during her cross-examination is peculiarly illuminating in more than one respect:

Did you tell your husband that you were buying clothes for Stoner?—I never told him that I was buying clothes even for little John.

You bought silk pyjamas at 60s. a suit?—That might seem absurd, but that is my disposition.

You have told us that on the Sunday night Stoner came into your bedroom and got into bed with you. That was something which happened frequently?—Oh, always.

Were you fond of your little boy John?—I love both my children.

Were you fond of John?—Naturally.

Did John sleep in the same room?—Yes, but in another bed on the other side of the room.

Not a very large room?—No, but little John was always asleep.

Are you suggesting to members of the jury that you, a mother, fond of her little boy of 6, was permitting this man to get into bed with you in the same room where your little innocent child was asleep?—I do not consider that that was frightful or dreadful.

The pluckiness no less than the honesty of that last answer is commendable. Mrs. Rattenbury did not, of course, consider her conduct frightful or dreadful, because it had been she who had ordered it, and she knew just how it had come about, how ordinary and inevitable it had been, how exceptional the circumstances were, and, therefore, how it had been anything but frightful or dreadful; though if she had been one of the ten million British wives and mothers who avidly read these words the next morning, and if the words and the circumstances had been somebody else's, Mrs. Rattenbury would doubtless have agreed with counsel for the prosecution that such a thing was both frightful and dreadful. (The more sophisticated readers would, perhaps, not mind the immorality so much as the bad taste.) As it was, however, the question (which we may hope was not intended as an incidental lesson in grammar) could only have been designed to show what a callous, inhuman, and abandoned fiend the prisoner must be; and Mrs. Rattenbury, instead of wriggling before his spear-thrust under her ribs, bravely accepted the challenge and replied, in effect, that counsel might think so but she did not.

With all the information which Mrs. Rattenbury's evidence afforded, we have already dealt; but there were one or two items not under this heading which may be quoted. It was plain that she had been thoroughly deceived by Stoner's drug-taking fantasy, and she denied with great emphasis that she had ever taken drugs herself. She showed considerable reluctance to speak of the wish her husband had expressed on the afternoon of March 24th to commit suicide. When counsel suggested that her feeling for Stoner was "just an infatuation", Mrs. Rattenbury replied: "I think it was more than that." "You fell in love with him?" asked counsel. "Absolutely," Mrs. Rattenbury answered. The word was her favourite one, and she used it often instead of a mere "Yes"; a little character-pointer which is not without its interest.

Here is another instance of the witness's honesty under cross-examination, even when speaking the truth might harm her own case:

Were you fond of your husband?—I did not love him; no.

If he had wanted his rights as a husband would you
have been ready to grant them to him in March 1935?—
No.

If counsel had hoped to elicit some damaging admissions
upon the significance of which he could afterwards enlarge,
he had it here handed to him on a plate, so openly that
perhaps the gift embarrassed rather than helped him.

Mr. O'Connor's examination concluded with the usual
meaningless question which defending counsel always put
to their clients, as if the assumption was that anyone would
rather confess to murder than commit perjury, and which
the newspapers the next morning always call "dramatic":

Did you yourself murder your husband?—Oh, no.
Did you take any part whatsoever in planning it?—
No.
Did you know anything about it until Stoner spoke
to you in your bed?—No. I would have prevented it
had I known a half or a quarter of a minute before—
naturally!

In this, as in the rest of her evidence, Mrs. Rattenbury
no doubt spoke the truth. In fact the only statements of hers
which seem open to any doubt are those in which she denied
any memory at all of everything that happened after she
was sick on the whisky she had drunk soon after finding
her husband wounded; and one would not be sceptical here
were the maxim not so well known that ignorance is the
best defence. Even so, Mrs. Rattenbury almost carries conviction:

I can remember a few things, like an awful nightmare. I remember rubbing his hands because they were
cold, and I wanted to get his teeth in for him to tell
me what had happened. And little John standing in the
doorway with his little face—I remember that. I re-

member getting into the car, but I don't know what car.

Finally, the judge himself put a few questions to Mrs. Rattenbury on this point, making clear to the jury her contention that she remembered perfectly what Stoner had said to her in bed, even down to the detail of hiding the mallet; it was only later that her memory failed.

"But you remember every word by Stoner just before?" persisted the judge.

"Yes, naturally," Mrs. Rattenbury replied. "I hadn't had that dreadful shock then. I was quite happy. Life was different."

Mr. Casswell was in a difficult position when he rose to open the case for Stoner, and he made no secret of his difficulties to the jury. He began with a reference to the case of Thompson and Bywaters, and warned the jury not to look on that case as a precedent for this one, for in that there was indisputable evidence that both the accused were present when the fatal blow was struck.

Mr. Casswell pointed out that the case for the Crown was one of conspiracy: two people were in the dock, and the prosecution averred that each was equally guilty with the other. Yet:

> Can you imagine any crime which bears less evidence of having been the result of two people working it out beforehand? It was the result of a sudden impulse—the mad act of one only.

> This is the position [pointed out counsel, as well he might]. The Crown accusing two people, and each one trying to take the blame on him—or herself: and one of them a cocaine addict whose statements cannot be relied upon. You can imagine that the defence of Stoner has been a very anxious task. You can imagine that few stones have been left unturned to find out what is the truth. Because if this had not been a joint trial—if

I could have been in the happy position of representing
Stoner and Stoner alone, I could have said boldly that
the prosecution have not proved their case: the evidence against this boy is practically nothing. But how
can I do that when there is someone else in the dock?

That counsel for Stoner intended to be very careful for
that other person in the dock he showed at once. Referring
further to the Thompson-Bywaters case, he said:

Many doubts have been expressed as to whether one
of those persons was rightly convicted. That is the sort
of thing you will be particularly careful to see does not
happen here. There must be no mistake.

This was tantamount to an admission from Stoner's counsel that Mrs. Rattenbury was innocent. The admission that
Stoner alone was responsible was a necessary corollary.
Having committed himself so far on his journey between
Scylla and Charybdis, Mr. Casswell then indicated what, in
these peculiar and perhaps unique circumstances, his defence was to be. Suggesting that a possible verdict in the
case of Stoner was "guilty, but insane", counsel offered them
what amounted to his own way out of the difficulty: that the
confusion in Stoner's mind was such, and the toxic effect of
the cocaine was such, that he was not capable of forming the
necessary intent to make the crime of murder. In other words,
he gave them the alternative of manslaughter.

I ask you [pleaded Mr. Casswell], when you have
heard the evidence, that in view of the facts of this
case and incidents of the crime, it is impossible to say
anybody did it in his normal mind.

(Even at the risk of breaking the narrative one must pause
here to wonder whether advocates really do use in their
speeches such peculiar grammar, or whether this is always
a fault in the reporting.)

This was about the best defence Stoner could make. It eliminated Mrs. Rattenbury from the crime and so might prevent a repetition of the Thompson-Bywaters blunder; and this altruism might not be without its own reward in the favourable impression it would make on the jury. Moreover, the elimination of Mrs. Rattenbury would have another good result for Stoner in removing the conspiracy to murder, which intensifies the degree of this crime so definitely. By saying, "Yes, he did it, the poor lad, maddened by jealousy and dulled by drugs, in a single mad moment," counsel was making the murder of Mr. Rattenbury a much more excusable act than the prosecution's version of an abandoned woman who would stick at nothing to obtain her sexual gratification, plotting with her brutal young lover to batter in a helpless old man's head. And in any case, to attempt to make Stoner out completely innocent would, in the face of Miss Riggs' evidence alone, have been hopeless.

The trial was adjourned in the middle of counsel's address, and on the next day, the fourth, Mr. Casswell proceeded to develop his plea by citing the recent successful appeal which he himself had made to the House of Lords in a case of murder, when the Lord Chancellor laid it down that when dealing with a murder case the Crown must prove: (*a*) death as the result of a voluntary act of the accused, and (*b*) malice on the part of the accused. In commenting on and explaining this dictum, Mr. Casswell stated the law on this point so clearly and interestingly as to deserve quotation in full:

> If the defence either from evidence given by the prosecution or from evidence called for the defence shows an explanation which, if true, would amount to a good defence, the onus of proof is still upon the prosecution to show that the defence is not true. But there is one exception, and it was clearly pointed out in the recent decision in the House of Lords. If the accused's defence is, "I did the act, but I had not suf-

ficient intent, owing to a disease of the mind, or to
drunkenness, or to the taking of drugs, which rendered
me in such a state that I was incapable of forming that
design,'' it is for the accused to prove that.

This, then, was the defence made on behalf of Stoner,
and to maintain it counsel had to prove that Stoner was a
drug-addict; a contention with which he had not had very
much success so far.

Mr. Casswell went on:

You have heard the evidence of Mrs. Rattenbury,
and on Stoner's behalf I accept and endorse the whole
of her explanation of the matters which led up to the
day of March 24th, and what happened on that day. It
necessarily follows that she, in my submission, did not
commit this act, and had nothing to do with it. The
prisoner Stoner does not deny—in fact, admits—that it
was his hand that struck the blow.

This was very fair. Indeed, the judge seemed to think
that it was too fair, and that counsel had gone beyond pro-
priety in making this admission. The newspapers naturally
seized upon it, and quite properly. We, the public, who
were trying this man and woman, of course were anxious
to know where the truth lay, so that we might be satisfied
that the condemnation or leniency as it might be of our
representatives, the jury, had been properly applied; and
our only way of learning such things is through the newspapers. To castigate these, as the learned judge did the next
day, for giving prominence to such a crux in the case, on
the grounds that they ''seem to regard this sort of terrible
tragedy as a godsend to them'', was not only giving one
half of the picture and that the smaller, but is an indication
of a rather unfortunate attitude of mind not uncommon
among our higher judiciary officials, that what goes on in
their courts concerns only those people actually taking part
in the proceedings and not at all the public in whose name

all trials are held, who appoint the officials to conduct them, and who in the persons of their representatives, the jury, decide the issue.

Mr. Casswell then concluded his very able speech by repeating the alternatives which he had suggested to the jury of "guilty, but insane," or manslaughter, with the reasons why they might arrive at either.

The Stoner parents were Mr. Casswell's first witnesses. Mr. Stoner testified to his son's weak physical condition, fainting fits, and general backwardness as a child, and Mrs. Stoner said that when he visited her early in the afternoon of March 24th, Stoner appeared quite normal. (Mr. Casswell later contrasted this normality with the scene Stoner made over the visit to Bridport.)

Counsel then got down to the real job, and called his two experts who were to prove that Stoner was a drug-addict.

The first was Dr. L. A. Weatherley, a mental expert and the president of the Society of Mental and Nervous Diseases. He had visited Stoner in Dorchester Prison, and though not prepared to say that Stoner was mentally deficient he was convinced that Stoner was a cocaine-addict. His conclusion was based on Stoner's description of the cocaine-addict's hallucination of touch, as being like a rash moving about under his skin. Dr. Weatherley, having made up his mind on the main point, naturally found that everything else fitted in, particularly the violent jealousy. Even the fact that Stoner possessed a small dagger was regarded by Dr. Weatherley as a symptom of addiction to cocaine, who also unspiked the gun disabled by Dr. Grierson by stating that after the exaltation of cocaine passed off it was followed by a feeling of great mental irritability.

All the incidents on Stoner's part after 4.30 on March 24th were put down by Dr. Weatherley to cocaine, particularly the threats and violence over the Bridport visit and the accusation of "relationship" (counsel's excellent word) by Mrs. Rattenbury with her husband when the bedroom door was closed in the afternoon, which the witness considered "entirely an hallucination of hearing arising out of cocainism".

The judge, who appears to have become a little restive under this sweeping positivism, then asked the witness whether all these incidents might also be consistent "with his not having taken a dose of cocaine, but being very angry and jealous with his mistress", to which Dr. Weatherley, sticking manfully by his artillery, replied, "I doubt it."

Mr. Casswell, indeed, must have deplored this continued scepticism on the part of the judge, for after further references to cocaine-induced jealousy we have the latter asking again: "Do you know after sixty-two years as a medical man that some people get very jealous without cocaine or drink having anything to do with it?" This time the witness had to cede a little ground and admit that he had heard of such disappointing cases.

As may be expected, Mr. Croom-Johnson got very little change out of this veteran in cross-examination, Dr. Weatherley definitely refusing to agree that cocaine-addicts get irritable and upset when deprived of the drug; morphia-addicts, heroin-addicts, any other addicts you like, yes, but cocaine-addicts, just as it happens, no.

Dr. Gillespie followed Dr. Weatherley into the witness-box.

Dr. Gillespie, the physician for psychological medicine at Guy's Hospital, explained the usual symptoms of the cocaine-addict, laying stress on the "morbid jealousy", under the domination of which a person is extremely likely to misinterpret all the goings-on around him.

Here the judge interposed, "Is that not true of all jealousy?"

Dr. Gillespie, who does not seem to have displayed the true British doggedness of Dr. Weatherley, hedged a little. "Yes, my lord, but I should have thought it more likely to happen in a diseased jealousy."

"Have you ever read the play of *Othello?*" asked the judge.

Dr. Gillespie hedged again. He had read it—but a long time ago.

This exchange seems to have thrown counsel as well as witness a little off his balance, for a few moments later Mr. Casswell asked what must be one of the most difficult questions ever put to a witness:

> Is a person at the moment of committing that act of violence likely to think much beforehand of the consequences?

Nevertheless, Dr. Gillespie was equal to this, and replied, in effect, that he did not believe that such a person would think much beforehand while in the act of committing violence; wherein the doctor was undoubtedly right.

A little later, when the possible regeneration of cocaine-addicts was under discussion, the judge took the business in hand again and, thrusting a pin through all the verbiage, pricked Mr. Casswell's pretty balloon with this unkind but pertinent question to the witness:

> Do you know in your experience any such case as this—a cocaine-addict suddenly cut off from any supply, given no drugs of any sort or kind to take the place of cocaine, and from the day that the supply is cut off, for a period of two months, being a person who could probably be described as rational, sleeping well, taking his food well, and being perfectly healthy?

Dr. Gillespie then had to admit that, on the whole, and perhaps with qualifications, he would be surprised to meet such a case.

That ended the expert evidence for the defence.

Those who expected Stoner to take his turn next in the box were disappointed. Mr. Casswell, rising to make his final address, explained that to put Stoner in the box could not help the jury at all, since he was under the influence of a drug at the time, and what he could say would be of little consequence. Nor had Mr. Casswell much new to say. He summed up the evidence he had called, and asked the jury to say that, from the time he threatened Mrs. Rattenbury at the telephone with a revolver, Stoner's acts were "not those of a normal boy, but the acts of somebody under the influence of insane hallucination". As for the contention of the prosecution that the murder had been planned and committed to get Mr. Rattenbury out of the way, "Whose way was he in?" asked Mr. Casswell.

One striking passage in Mr. Casswell's speech sums up nearly everything that we feel to be strange, and therefore wrong, about this case:

> In my submission the only motive that can be assigned was entirely unsufficient for this crime. It was simply the motive to prevent the trip to Bridport.
>
> You get this clumsy crime, committed in this clumsy manner, with no chance of an alibi, no attempt at escape, no chance of the defence of accident, no chance of pleading that it was suicide.
>
> By all these considerations you are driven, and inevitably driven, to the conclusion that this was an act of impulse, the act of somebody who had not planned it beforehand, who acted under an impulse—as I suggest, an uncontrollable impulse.

Much of this is true. The crime was certainly one of the most stupid murders ever committed. Yet it is possible to believe that Mrs. Casswell's "inevitable conclusion" contains only half the truth.

Repeating his offer of guilty but insane or manslaughter, Mr. Casswell sat down.

Mr. Croom-Johnson summed up the case for the prosecution very temperately. He suggested that the key to the solution of the problem was that "Stoner throughout this unhappy story was dominated by Mrs. Rattenbury", and asked whether it was possible to believe the word of a woman "who, upon her own statement, has for some years been engaged in lying to her husband about money matters". He cast doubt on Mrs. Rattenbury's assertion that her mind went blank, and said that it was his duty, on behalf of the prosecution, to suggest to the jury that the statements in which Mrs. Rattenbury had incriminated herself were the truth. Mr. Croom-Johnson also laid stress on the exchange between Mrs. Rattenbury and Stoner as the former was leaving the house under arrest; he described this evidence as "of the greatest significance in the case", and asked the jury whether it did not indicate to them that the two prisoners had had a common object that night.

Mr. Croom-Johnson was dealing with Mr. Casswell's suggestion of a verdict of guilty but insane, when the judge intervened to say that he intended to tell the jury not only that such a verdict would be justified, but that they must put out of their minds Mr. Casswell's admission that it had been Stoner who struck the blows. "They must decide the case on the evidence and not on any quasi-admission his counsel may make. Stoner has not said so," remarked the judge.

Mr. Croom-Johnson concluded his speech with a remarkable sentence, in which he deliberately allowed the human being to show through the mask of duty:

But if, and perhaps mercifully in pursuance of your oath, you can still bring yourselves to the view that you are not satisfied that a case has been made out to your satisfaction, then it will be your duty—and, possibly, a pleasure to us all—for you to say, not being satisfied, that your verdict is a verdict for the defence.

This was the clearest possible hint to the jury that the prosecution, though dutifully putting forward such evidence as there was against Mrs. Rattenbury, were not really pressing the case against her—and might even be grateful for an acquittal.

Mr. O'Connor began his address for Mrs. Rattenbury with a tribute to the fairness with which the prosecution had been conducted, as well he might. Counsel did not spare the moral character of his client, but warned the jury that this must not mean "that justice is to be prostituted because you have been misled, because of your hatred of the life she has been leading"; and he pointed out, rightly, that without her own statements there was no evidence against Mrs. Rattenbury at all. "Fragments snatched from the disordered mind of a woman sodden with drink and hysteria," was Mr. Connor's unflattering but graphic description of his client's confession.

Counsel for the defence came perhaps nearer the mark than counsel for the prosecution when he spoke of Mrs. Rattenbury as a woman "who, by her own acts and folly, had erected in the boy a Frankenstein of jealousy which she could not control". Disregarding the incorrectness of the literary allusion, this is more like the truth than that the key to the solution of the problem was Mrs. Rattenbury's domination of Stoner. One does not dominate what one cannot control, and there is plenty of indication in the evidence that Mrs. Rattenbury could not by any means control Stoner. A woman of that type, too, revels in being dominated.

Mr. O'Connor made this handsome reference to Stoner:

Stoner has played a gentleman's part. You may possibly think that he has atoned for a great deal by refusing to commit the supreme crime of seeing his mistress go to her doom for a crime which he knows he committed.

It may, indeed, have been this plea, even more than anything Stoner's own counsel said, which influenced the jury's verdict.

With the end of Mr. O'Connor's speech the proceedings of the fourth day concluded.

On the Friday morning Mr. Justice Humphreys began his summing-up.

Beginning in the usual way by explaining the law as it bears upon two persons agreeing together to commit a felony, the judge remarked that his five days' experience of the case had satisfied him that he had been right in deciding that the two defendants should be tried together. Then, having dealt with such facts as were common to both prisoners, he proceeded to consider the case of Mrs. Rattenbury.

In view of the fact that upon many important matters Mrs. Rattenbury was the only person to have given evidence (said the judge), it was essential for the jury to make up their minds whether they believed her evidence or not; and that would depend to some extent on the kind of woman they considered her to be. This is much the same as Mr. Justice Shearman said in his summing-up in the Thompson case, and is a proper use of evidence concerning character. But whereas the judge in the Thompson-Bywaters case allowed the jury to gather that in his opinion a woman who could be guilty of adultery could just as well be guilty of murder—that the step, in fact, from adultery to murder was only a small one—Mr. Justice Humphreys was evidently not going to have any share for his own part in yet another British condemnation for adultery on a charge of murder. Let us salute the first British judge who has definitely warned a jury against our own particular national injustice (does it arise out of priggishness, sadism, or womanly influence?) in these plain words:

> Having heard your own counsel with regard to the facts of this case, it may be you will say that you cannot possibly feel any sympathy with this woman. You cannot possibly have any feeling except of disgust for her. But let me say this: that should not make you more ready to convict her of this crime. It should, if anything, make you less ready to accept evidence against her, if you think there can be any explanation consistent with her innocence. But I know you will not let it prejudice you against her. So far as it is material evidence in this case, you must use it. If you think it shows the sort of woman who might have the motive to do this thing, then you must use it because it is admissible evidence. But beware that you do not con-

vict her of this crime because she is an adulteress—
and an adulteress, you may think, of the most unpleasant type.

This is very fair; very fair indeed. One may, perhaps,
have all sorts of feelings for Mrs. Rattenbury besides disgust, but still—Mrs. Maybrick had been convicted of murder upon a single instance of adultery and a suspicion; Mrs.
Thompson had been executed for adultery. Mr. Justice
Humphreys, at any rate, did not intend to add to the list of
these victims of the British Courts of Morals.

This was an innovation indeed. So far from safeguarding
justice as the written law defines it, most judges in the past
have gone out of the way to inflame the jury to condemn on
the moral issue instead of the legal one. Contrast, for instance, the more reasonable of Mr. Justice Humphreys'
words with a passage from the summing-up against Mrs.
Thompson (the preposition is used advisedly):

> Just at the end of a letter I shall have to allude to
> again, comes this: "He has the right by law to all that
> you have the right to by nature and love." Gentlemen,
> if that nonsense means anything it means that the love
> of a husband for his wife is something improper be-
> cause marriage is acknowledged by the law, and that
> the love of a woman for her lover, illicit and clandes-
> tine, is something great and noble. I am certain that
> you, like any other right-minded persons, will be filled
> with disgust at such a notion.

Alas, that is more like the attitude of our national judiciary which, set to try human beings who have lived and
loved as their natures dictated and not with their noses in
the statute-books, are either utterly ignorant of human nature
or else deliberately disregard it. Could not every judge, before he is allowed to take his seat on the bench, be put
through a short course, followed by an examination in psychology, love and plain ordinary cussed human nature?

Then, perhaps, they might not make such egregious observations.

Although he was careful to add the rider of warning, Mr. Justice Humphreys showed that he fully shared this conventional legal attitude both in his unchristian reference to disgust for the woman caught out in adultery, and in pronouncing that adulterous relations "lack the one thing that makes for ordinary peaceable happiness between married couples, and that is respect". To say that respect cannot exist between a man and woman whose relations are legally improper is just as silly as to say that respect invariably exists between married couples. Marriage does not make for the one nor adultery for the other, which may be legally and even socially regrettable, but is true.

As to Stoner, the judge pointed out that the jury

> had no more right to give effect to evidence in his case from motives of pity than you have the right to refuse to give effect to evidence in her case which may be in her favour, because you thoroughly despise her. It is a pitiable thing that you should have been brought to this pass, and I do not think I am putting it unfairly even against her when I say that, whatever your verdict may be in the case, his position is due to the domination of this woman.

This, whether fair or not, is certainly arguable.

The judge then tried hard to persuade the jury that counsel for Stoner had not said what he did say, or, if he had said it, had not meant it.

> A little mistake was made by those who thought that Mr. Casswell intended to say that his client admitted striking the blow. It would have been quite improper for counsel who was not going to call evidence, to say anything of the sort, and it is not what Mr. Casswell meant at all. All he meant was that its being the case of the prosecution that they had to prove that it was

Stoner who struck the blow, he was in the position, or
at all events did not intend, to call evidence to contra-
dict, and therefore did not propose to address you on
that part of the case. He had therefore to leave it there.
That is all he meant.

As I rather expected, I noticed those newspapers
which seem to regard this sort of terrible tragedy as a
godsend to them, have found one thing and one thing
only to put on their posters, and that was "Stoner's
counsel said he committed the crime."

As, however, Mr. Casswell's exact words, as reported,
were "Stoner does not deny—in fact, admits—that his hand
struck the blow," the newspapers apparently were right and
the learned judge wrong. The parenthesis may have been
unfortunate, but there it was; and a million British homes
were quite rightly relieved to know the truth.

Mr. Justice Humphreys was on more fertile ground when
he passed on to Stoner's alleged drug-taking. Without precisely ridiculing it, and indeed treating it quite fairly, he
gave the jury plainly to understand his opinion that this was
all bunkum. He pointed out the absence in prison of all the
symptoms usual to drug-addicts; he made a very reasonable
point in reminding the jury that Mrs. Rattenbury had said
nothing of Stoner appearing abnormal or under the influence of a drug when he told her in bed what he had done,
and he put forward for their consideration this significant
suggestion:

Now here I am bound to point out to you something
which you may think is the most important fact about
this matter, and perhaps is conclusive. There is one
human being who knows whether Stoner was in the
habit of taking cocaine or whether he was not, or
whether he took it that afternoon. That person is Stoner
himself. He is an admissible and available witness, and
if he wishes, or those who defend him wish, to prove
that he is or was addicted to drugs, had taken cocaine

or was under the influence of cocaine, is there any
witness on earth who could do it as well as Stoner? It
seems to me, in the circumstances of this case, a fact
of most profound significance that Stoner prefers not
to give evidence.

This was a legitimate comment on the part of the judge,
and is true enough, though it might be that Stoner, who, if
he went into the witness-box to prove himself a cocaine-
addict, would lay himself open to all sorts of other questions
too, had further awkward secrets to keep hidden.

As to the plea of guilty but insane, the judge would have
none of it; there was no evidence to justify it, and without
such evidence the issue could not be left to the jury at all.

Lastly, Mr. Justice Humphreys commented on the "statement" made by Mrs. Rattenbury in the morning, while she
was still muddled by morphia. Saying that he had no power
to withdraw this statement from the evidence, the judge
hinted very strongly to the jury to take no notice of it. "It
seems to me to be . . . not quite acting with the fairness
which, I suppose, one may say is characteristic of our criminal courts," he remarked, with a kind of suave bluntness.

The judge then went through certain portions of the evidence in detail, and concluded after speaking for three and
a half hours. His summing-up was not only absolutely fair
throughout, but in places masterly; and one hopes that other
judges will profit by it.

The jury were absent for about an hour. The verdicts
were: Mrs. Rattenbury not guilty, Stoner guilty, with a recommendation to mercy. The recommendation in Stoner's
case was presumably due to his youth and to the jury's belief, following the expressed opinions of the judge and
counsel for the prosecution that he had been under the domination of Mrs. Rattenbury.

When asked if he had anything to say before sentence of
death was passed, Stoner stood firmly erect and replied, in
a low but steady voice: "Nothing at all."

Mr. Justice Humphreys then passed sentence, saying that

the jury's recommendation would be forwarded to the proper quarter, and Stoner was taken back to prison.

Mrs. Rattenbury, who had been waiting, still in custody, in the corridor below while Stoner was being sentenced, was then called back to the court. As the wardress was helping her towards the short flight of stone stairs which leads to the dock, she met Stoner face to face as he was hurried past. They exchanged a silent look. Did each of them know it was the last?

Mrs. Rattenbury was kept standing in the dock for a few minutes while the officials discussed whether or not to proceed with a second indictment charging her with being an accessory after the fact, knowing that Stoner "had wounded with intent to murder". Mrs. Rattenbury now looked tired and worn. Finally, it was announced that the prosecution would offer no evidence, and Mrs. Rattenbury was formally discharged.

The trial had been followed with great interest by the population as a whole, and the verdicts were received with relief. In the minds of most citizens the injustice done to Mrs. Thompson remained as a little lump of uneasiness, and there was a general feeling, which the judge and counsel for the prosecution interpreted, that a similar injustice must not be allowed to occur in the case of Mrs. Rattenbury.

It was this feeling which added the extra sharpness to the popular interest in the trial, but even without it there was plenty of reason for interest. Superior persons deprecate this interest in murder trials as morbid, or sensation-seeking; judges openly resent it; yet if one faces the corollary, it is difficult to see how any normal person can remain indifferent to a trial such as this, and its result. One might go so far as to throw the challenge to the superior persons that actually it is the interest which is normal and indifference abnormal.

For quite apart from the responsibility which, in a take-it-for-granted, undefined, perhaps unrecognized way, we, the people, feel as any democracy should feel concerning

those who are being tried in our name and by our chosen
representatives (so that any mishap to justice is not a thing
apart from us, but brings shame on each individual man or
woman among us), there is the common humanity which
draws each of us towards another human being in prolonged
peril of life. Here the popular interest in a murder trial is
akin to that with which the account is followed of a disabled
ship floundering in a distant sea. Will it keep afloat till the
rescuers reach it, or will it sink? We know nothing of the
men on board; we do not even know their names; but—will
they live or die? This, too, explains why the interest aroused
by a trial for murder is so much greater than that aroused
by the most notorious of crooked financiers; and not only
greater, but different, for it exists on a higher plane in the
human mentality.

That it can exist simultaneously on a lower plane is not
to be disputed, for we must admit that, spicing this interest
in a rescue at sea no less than in a trial for murder, there is
a minute pinch of sadism: nothing abnormal and only in
proportion to the minute pinch of sadism which is common
to nearly all of us, but there it is. It is, however, only when
this pinch becomes a handful, so that there is positive gloat-
ing over the agonies which the accused must be enduring,
that interest in a murder trial can be called morbid, which
means diseased, or even sensation-mongering; and that
surely can only happen in very few instances.

Then there is what, for want of a more precise term, may
be called "scientific" interest. This is the appeal exercised
by the detective-story, in distinction to the thriller, the appeal of the puzzle, the wish to know the truth.

"Why," I asked myself when I began to write this account, "does this case interest you so much? Why do so
many murder-cases interest you so much? Why do others
not interest you at all? Are you morbid?"

"No," I replied indignantly to myself, "I am not morbid, and if you'll let me think a minute I'll answer you.
Yes, I am interested on two main counts; as a student of
character I am interested in the minds which, whether

through attributes or deficiencies as the case may show, can first envisage murder as a practical solution of their difficulties and then, which is much rarer, turn this vision into action—in other words, I suppose, since most interests have an egotistical basis, as a psychological mechanic, if I may so describe myself to you, I am interested to compare these engines of the human chassis with my own, so like and yet, I sincerely hope, so unlike; and secondly, I have a sneaking passion for the truth, and when *A* says one thing and *B* another and the fact that *C* seems to prove both of them wrong, I will hunt the real truth through acres of examination, cross-examination, advocacy, summing-up, and other rough country, till I can feel satisfied that I have made my kill. Those are my two chief reasons, and as a minor one I can cite the interest I feel in the lives of other people and how they are lived, and nothing outside fiction so effectually knocks down the front wall of a house and exposes its occupants in the details of their strange lives as does a trial for murder.''

Those who, as spectators, follow a murder trial, not in the newspapers but in court, have recorded not without surprise that they found themselves paying very little attention to the prisoners in the dock. The fact that a life is dependent on the way the game is played, and the winning of it, is lost in the game itself. The efforts to dig out the truth, the efforts sometimes to conceal it, the vast attention paid to the rules under which the truth is to be sought as if the rules were more important than the truth itself, the manœuvring and counter-manœuvring inside those rules, the bull-fighters with their red flags and their higher intelligences cajoling, goading, or tricking the unwitting bulls of witnesses into the required position until zip! goes the sword, and the witness is pinned to the arena with an admission or a contradiction; these things hold the attention of the onlooker. It is the interest of technique, and in court is seems to be paramount.

Political responsibility, common humanity, a pinch of sadism, desire to know the truth, psychology, life as it is lived by others, the technique of justice, and lastly, the determination of organized society to exact retribution for wrong-doing, these are the seven chief heads of the complicated, instinctive, popular interest in a trial for murder, and not one of them is abnormal. With the possible exception of the third, not one of them is even morbid.

Stoner had passed through his ordeal apparently unmoved. Through the whole five days of the trial he had shown no emotion, just as he had shown none after the murder. His face a little pale, his manner stolid, with a faintly sullen set to his mouth, he allowed no one to guess whether it was indifference, courage, resignation, or sheer inability to feel as other people do, that was holding him up. Mrs. Rattenbury had been slowly disintegrating under the eyes of the jury. During the long summing-up she had sat for the most part without moving a muscle; when she took up a glass of water it was with the mechanical action of a marionette.

Mrs. Rattenbury was not to profit by having been tried by a sensible judge and an intelligent jury. The ordeal had been too much for her certainly unbalanced temperament. On the third day after the acquittal she entered a London nursing-home for rest and treatment. At about 3.30 the next afternoon, of Tuesday June 4th, she borrowed £2 from one of the officials of the home and went out, after telling the matron that she would be back by nine o'clock. She appeared to the matron to be in a normal state of bodily health, and since the doctor had said she could go out neither the matron nor anyone else had the power to detain her.

From 3.30 p.m. there is a five-hours' blank. Then, at 8.30 p.m. on the same day a labourer, walking through a meadow near Christchurch, Bournemouth, saw a woman sitting on the opposite bank of a stream, a backwater of the Avon, near the place where a railway arch passed over it. She was alone, and was smoking a cigarette. The labourer noticed next, as he walked on, that there was a knife in the woman's hand, and as he looked at her he saw her tumble forward into the water. The man had to run up the bank on his own side of the stream, over the bridge, and down the other side. When he reached her, the woman was lying face upwards in the water a few feet from the bank. The labourer, who could not swim, waded out as far as he dared, but could not reach her, so snatched up her fur coat, which was lying on the bank and threw the end of it towards her, but the woman made no attempt to catch it. The man then saw that there was blood in the water, and as he could do no more for her he ran to a cottage near by for help. It was now about 8.40 p.m.

Collecting a second man, and a pole, the rescuer hurried back, but the pole was too short and they could do nothing. The first man then went to notify the police, while the second went back to his cottage for a longer pole. With this he was able to pull the body ashore, and when a policeman arrived at 9 p.m. he found it lying on the bank. A few yards away was a handbag, containing a number of letters, and a paper bag in which was a dagger-sheath. The body was identified later as that of Mrs. Rattenbury.

Examined by a doctor the next morning, the body showed six stab-wounds in the chest, five large and one small. Five of the wounds were in the left breast, all passing downwards and inwards, and of these no less than three had penetrated the heart, one of them making a large cut through which the instrument had apparently passed more than once. The doctor considered that death must have been almost instantaneous and that Mrs. Rattenbury would have been dead before she reached the water.

At the inquest which was held on the following Friday, June 6th, at Christchurch, extracts were read from the letters Mrs. Rattenbury had left. The first was from a letter dated June 4th:

> I want to make it perfectly clear that no one is responsible for what action I may take regarding my life. I quite made up my mind at Holloway to finish things should Stoner . . . and it would only be a matter of

time and opportunity. Every night and minute is only prolonging the appalling agony of my mind.

At this point the coroner broke off, saying: "Then this goes into quite a lot of neurotic statements." One would have thought that these neurotic statements would have been valuable evidence as to the deceased's state of mind, but nothing more from this letter was read.

The next extract came from a letter addressed to "The Governor of His Majesty's Prison, Pentonville," and ran:

If I only thought it would help Stoner I would stay on, but it has been pointed out to me all too vividly I cannot help him. That is my death sentence.

Another passage had been written on the back of an old envelope:

Eight o'clock. After so much walking I have got here. Oh, to see the swans and spring flowers, and just smell them. And how singular I should have chosen the spot Stoner said he nearly jumped out of the train once at.

It was not intentional my coming here. I tossed a coin like Stoner always did, and it came down Christchurch. It is beautiful here. What a lovely world we are in. It must be easier to be hanged than to have to do the job oneself, especially in these circumstances of being watched all the while.

Pray God nothing stops me to-night. Am within five minutes of Christchurch now. God bless my children and look after them.

Another extract, written the same evening, read:

I tried this morning to throw myself under a train at Oxford Circus. Too many people about. Then a 'bus. Still too many people about. One must be bold to do

a thing like this. It is beautiful here and I am alone.
Thank God for peace at last.

For once there was justification for that stereotyped verdict, suicide during temporary insanity, designed in true
British compromise to get round an obsolete law and so save
anyone the bother of repealing it. By this time Mrs. Rattenbury, if still not legally insane, was for all practical considerations so. The egomania of the neurotic pushed aside even
her children's claims upon her life. She could not await the
result of Stoner's appeal. Since *she* could not save him, she
would die; whether anyone else might save him, seems
hardly to have interested her. It was not Stoner, it was herself whom she was concerned about, to the end. She probably never wondered whether her death could be the least
use to anyone, even to herself; it was the grand, the final
gesture, and if there was a touch of exhibitionism and more
than a touch of melodrama about it, well, that was only in
character. The method she chose, surely unique in the an-
nals of feminine suicide, not only shows the determination
which her mania had lent her, but seems to convey a masochistic hint; and that, too, would only be in character.

So ended Mrs. Rattenbury, who had done a great deal of
harm in her forty years of life, performed an unnecessary
number of foolish actions, and been a great nuisance to
many people; an anti-social creature, incapable of seeing
any point of view but her own, and hag-ridden by her own
lusts; but, nevertheless, a woman more deserving of pity
than of the easy contempt she was forced to receive, and to
be admired insofar as that, within the limits of the nature
which she hardly tried to control, she was capable of the
generous gesture and even of a certain nobility. Of many
women who have never caused a murder, less could be said.

On June 25th Stoner's appeal was dismissed, the Lord
Chief Justice calling it a waste of time.

The fact [he said], if it be a fact, that a lad of good
character has been corrupted by an abandoned woman

old enough to be his mother, raises no question of law such as can be employed as a ground of appeal in this court.

The appeal had been made on the technical ground that there should have been separate trials, and that a joint trial involved the risk of a serious miscarriage of justice. There are sound arguments for this, but as a ground of appeal it was hopeless, both precedent and the law leaving no loophole for argument, however reasonable. As a secondary consideration, it was suggested that not enough importance had been attached by Mr. Justice Humphreys to "the defence of cocaine" ("Cocaine is not a defence," interrupted Lord Hewart. "It is a substance.") and that Stoner should now be heard as a witness on his own behalf.

Not unnaturally the Lord Chief Justice would have none of this. He described it as a cynical request, and said, rightly enough, that "there are no such exceptional circumstances here as would justify this court in permitting Stoner now, upon further consideration, to offer himself as a witness". Lord Hewart did not add, though he may have had the thought in mind, "Now that he has had time to receive a little coaching to the effect that cocaine is not a brown powder with black spots." He did add, however, that "if there is any observation to be made of the summing-up on this point, it is that Mr. Justice Humphreys treated with almost excessive respect the suggestion put to the jury". In other words the Court of Appeal no more believed that Stoner had been taking cocaine than did the judge in the court below: and, one must add, than any reasonable person could.

That the appeal would be dismissed must have seemed to Stoner's advisers inevitable. However, another string was being pulled at the same time, and shortly before the appeal was heard, a petition for Stoner's reprieve containing (it was said) 320,000 signatures, had been presented to the Home Secretary. There was considerable feeling in favour of a reprieve, and in this case the petition was not, as these petitions often are, at variance with public opinion. An important London newspaper voiced its own views—which means that it hoped it was voicing the views of its readers—in a leading article thus:

> We do not think it is putting it too high to say that public opinion is shocked at the idea that the ghastly drama in which this wretched boy has been involved must be rounded off by his death. We hope the Home Secretary will make a merciful decision without delay.

It is perhaps a little euphemistic to describe the bashing of a defenceless, drunken old man's head in with a mallet, apparently borrowed for the purpose, as a ghastly drama "in which this wretched boy has been involved", but this was an accurate interpretation of the public's opinion of the case at that time. Mrs. Rattenbury was the villain of it, not Stoner.

However that may be, the Home Secretary, Sir John Simon, who, being a really clever man, no doubt had his ear to the ground as every politician should and so few have, complied with the public's demand, and within twenty-four hours of the dismissal of his appeal, issued Stoner's reprieve, commuting his sentence to that of penal servitude for life. This means that Stoner, if his conduct is good, will be back among us in about fifteen years.

How does murder come about? How does it happen that an apparently decent, even lovable youth, can take a mallet and bang a defenceless, drunken old man on the head with it, intending that he shall die?

Before we can answer this question we have to determine so far as we can whether Stoner did intend that Mr. Rattenbury should die: and if he did so intend, over how long a period this intention had existed prior to the striking of the blows. On this vital matter there is very little evidence.

Perhaps the most helpful pointer is Stoner's statement to Miss Riggs when asked if his finger-prints would be found on the mallet: "No, I wore gloves." If it is true that Stoner had worn gloves and did not say this merely to impress Miss Riggs with his cleverness, in accordance with the vanity usual in criminals, this statement is surely decisive: it can only mean that Stoner did intend to kill Mr. Rattenbury, and was not merely trying to give him a painful tap or two to stop him from going to Bridport the next day and either saw red or underestimated his own strength, for we have evidence that the blows were delivered with considerable violence.

It is true that no finger-prints were found on the mallet, though it is equally true that the surface of the handle was not suitable for them; and there seems no reason to disbelieve this remark of Stoner's. Assuming then that he did wear gloves, this proves premeditation and malice extending at least over several minutes; and once premeditation is proved at all, the possibilities are open to any extension of the period. As evidence here, we have the borrowing of the mallet.

The mallet seems to have been borrowed round about eight o'clock on the evening of the murder. Stoner gave as his excuse that he wanted to drive in some tent-pegs in the garden. The validity or not of this pretext is crucial, and one can only repeat that it is surprising not to be able to find, in the reports of the trial, a single question put to Miss Riggs on this point. It seems, however, to have been assumed by all sides that the excuse was not a genuine one, and if we make the same assumption we get the premeditation-period put back at any rate to somewhere near the time of the upset over the journey to Bridport, which seems to have occurred round about six o'clock.

Is this, then, the end of the hunt? Was it the insane jealousy that Stoner showed over this trial matter which, kept at white heat for nearly four hours, caused him to murder Mr. Rattenbury that same evening, with the full knowledge of what he was doing and the full intention to do it? This was Stoner's own counsel's submission, and it may be true. It may, on the other hand, be only part of the truth.

There is this at any rate to be said for it. The crime was

an almost unbelievably stupid one, and unless Stoner was
simply half-witted he must have known that he had no
chance at all of escape. The only sane way of explaining
such an imbecile action is that it must have been committed
on the impulse of the moment, without time for reflection.
Yet we seem to have proved that the crime was not committed on the impulse of the moment, but after premeditation, extending over at least four hours, which is a long
time. Have we then to reconcile two irreconcilables before
we can suggest any explanation of how Mr. Rattenbury's
death came about?

I think we have not. We have been considering single-
track reasons, and human motives are seldom so simple and
uncomplicated as the courts have to pretend. Stoner did not
quite act on impulse, nor yet did he carry out what was a
cold-blooded, fully premeditated murder; and to understand
what really was in his mind, we must pay some attention to
the unwitting inspiration of his crime, Mrs. Rattenbury.

We have seen that Mrs. Rattenbury was a temperamental
lady; we have been told on the highest authority that she
was a wicked one. But for a proper estimate of her it cannot
be too much emphasized that, if she was a wicked woman,
she was an unconsciously wicked one: and we will leave it
to the ethicists to determine whether actual wickedness can
be anything but conscious. In any case Mrs. Rattenbury
certainly would never have thought of herself as a bad
woman, or as leading an immoral life, or indeed as anything
that she ought not to have been. These things are so different when it is we ourselves who are the centre of the picture,
and not some stranger. A faculty for detached self-analysis
is rare, and quite a high degree of it is required before a
woman can rise, scantily clad, from a lover's lap, a glass in
one hand and a cigarette in the other, and remark: ''Well,
well, I suppose this is an orgy, and I am an improper person
to be taking part in it.''

The excuses—more, the very excellent reasons, which
come rushing at once in support of our behaviour do not
merely cloud such clear-sightedness: they forestall it. That

these excuses do not hold good for other people in quite the same way, is merely natural. We should be poor creatures if we did not each one of us consider ourselves thoroughly and peculiarly different from the mass of other people.

Just as Mrs. Rattenbury would never have thought of herself as a bad woman, so she would never have looked on herself as an ordinary person. She would have recognised with pride how much more sensitive, more highly strung, more finely balanced she was than anyone else. And therefore she would take it for granted that the rules of conduct which apply to other and ordinary people, did not apply to her: a trait which the neurotics and the egocentrical hysterics share with the true criminal type. Not indeed that Mrs. Rattenbury would ever have reasoned the thing out, even in this simple way. She would have just taken it for granted that she was an exceptional, but certainly not an immoral woman.

Nor would it have occurred to her that she might be doing Stoner any *harm*. We may give her the benefit of the doubt and believe her that she was deceived at first in Stoner's age. When she learned how young he was, she tried to break things off: not because of any harm to Stoner, but probably for the sake of her own pride. Stoner, however, would not let her, and perhaps she did not try very hard. Afterwards she fell in love with him, and believed him to be in love with her: and how (she would think) can anything be wrong, or harmful, between two people who love? Nevertheless, it is my reading of Mrs. Rattenbury that, if anyone could have convinced her during this period that she really was doing Stoner harm, and that his association with herself was the worst possible thing for him, she would have given him up at once—if Stoner would have allowed himself to be given up.

As for the academic question of whether the association of a young man with a woman considerably older than himself is to be regarded always as harmful to the young man, that is debatable. The issue is usually confused, because so often the woman is married, but the court seemed to take it for granted that any such association is a terrible thing in itself, quite irrespective of what is to come out of it owing to the abnormality of one or other, or both, of the parties: and not only the association of a middle-aged married woman with a young man, but that between a young man and any "woman old enough to be his mother".

There is a case against the former, of course, because adultery is involved, and adultery, if not a legal crime, is a sin; so that any such relationship must be sinful, and therefore the parties to it must be guilt-conscious. In that, and in the lesson to disregard the marriage-bond, is where the harm lies for the younger delinquent. The flaw in this argument is that the parties never are guilt-conscious; and if there is no consciousness of guilt, we have to rule out the adjective invariably applied in court to a love-story of this kind, "sordid". We have to go further, too, and recognize that many of these extra-marital love affairs between middle-aged wives and young men are, at any rate so far as the young men are concerned, of an idealism rarely reached in plain, hum-drum, legal marriage. And without necessarily defending the women in such cases, only too often they have, or think that they have, plenty of justification, just as Mrs. Rattenbury herself had on more count than one. In any case to label these affairs as "nonsense" and "disgusting" is to shirk the problem; but judges and juries seem to enclose themselves in a little moral world of their own, to which the difficulties and complexities of real life are simply not admitted. No doubt they have to do so.

This, however, is not a discussion on the ethics of adulterous relations between a young man and a middle-aged wife, but on the much simpler question of whether an association with an older woman does a young man any actual harm. It is an important question in this case, for it was the only thing of which Mrs. Rattenbury was found guilty; indeed one might even say that it was the only charge seriously brought against her. It is no less important outside this case, for though judges and juries may throw up official hands of horror when an instance is brought under their noses, many of them must be guiltily conscious of very similar episodes in their own pasts. For the fact is that such an affair is by no means a rarity; it is, on the other hand, quite common, and there are few men who have not had some experience of it. Just as there are plenty of men who try to seduce girls, so there are plenty of women who are ready to initiate youths. The sexes are more on a par than is usually pretended.

And the harm to the youth? The current cant, of course, is to talk about the woman "leading the young man astray". That seems to suppose that, but for this woman, the young man would have no experience at all before marriage. Yet of how many men can this be said? And if he is to have experience, which initiation is the less harmful, at the hands of a woman like this or from a harlot? Provided the young man keeps his head, the question answers itself; and since the thing is going on now, this minute, in thousands of cases, one may assume that on the whole the young men do keep their heads. Even though adultery is involved, there is a certain idealism which is infinitely better than the sordidness inseparable from the harlot; and one may even say that nearly every young man who is given his initiation in this way is a victim saved from the harlots later, for having found what sexual experience combined with idealism can be, he is not likely ever to be satisfied with the one without the latter. To this extent, therefore, one may say that the association with an older woman, so far from doing the young man any "harm", does him a great deal of good.

If then the situation as between Mrs. Rattenbury and Stoner was, in its essentials, not at all an uncommon one, how was it that in this particular instance it led to murder?

The answer is, as in every question in which human beings and not algebraic symbols are involved, the characters of the two parties.

In Mrs. Rattenbury there was no malice, but there was a great deal of foolishness. Unfortunately foolishness can often do more harm than malice itself.

If it is the foolish driver or pedestrian who is responsible for 90 per cent of the road accidents, it is the foolish woman who must be blamed ultimately for most murders. Often she gets murdered herself, and usually she well deserves it. In other cases she is the incitement, often unconscious but none the less deadly. Even in cases of murder for gain a silly woman is generally mixed up in it somewhere: as extravagant wife, as greedy mistress, as accomplice, instigator, or victim. Outside fiction it is comparatively rare to find man murdering man for cold-blooded gain, as Palmer murdered Cook, or Lamson his nephew, without an unbalanced woman somewhere in the background to add a tinge of warmth to the affair.

It was the foolishness of Mrs. Rattenbury which led directly to Stoner's murder of her husband. One may wonder indeed that this particular situation, when a foolish woman is involved, does not lead to murder more often, with impressionable lads taking every silly word she says as angel's truth and looking on the unfortunate husband as a devil not fit to be alive. Apparently our youths are able to keep their heads even under the provocation of a Mrs. Rattenbury. And as for Mrs. Rattenbury, she would be alive to-day if the youth of her choice had not been a Stoner.

For Mrs. Rattenbury's type, though it may not be common, is unfortunately not rare enough. Most of us have met it at one time or another; and those who have, will not find it difficult to imagine something of what must have been going on at the Villa Madeira during January and February 1935. (The reconstruction would, actually, be easier if Stoner had been of the Bywaters type, idealistic, warmhearted, and impulsive. The probability that Stoner killed, in the end, more from a selfish than altruistic motive, complicates the emotional atmosphere.)

In assessing any type of woman, one must consider her under four heads: first, the self she shows to the world; second, the self she shows to her lover; third, the self which she either foists upon or exposes to herself according whether she is honest or dishonest, clear-sighted or myopic with herself; and fourthly, the true self that she really is.

Sometimes two of these selves coincide, perhaps in the rarest cases of utter honesty three, but no one except a saint can show the world the true self as one honestly knows it to be.

Of these four selves the one which causes the trouble with the Alma-Rattenbury type is the third. Such women see themselves as unique, important, misunderstood, and, generally, ill-used; and they are obsessed with themselves and their own peculiar agonies. Indeed, to a woman of this kind, herself is the only subject of any real importance. Their intimate talk tends entirely to their own self-glorification, and much of it is devoted to the exceptional sufferings they have undergone; and the more their listeners appear impressed, the more they pile on the agony.

So wrapped up in their pet subject are they, that to a lover they come perilously near exposing their true selves, vain, self-centred, shallow, full of distortions, and with the self-chosen, masochistic squirmings of the pseudo-martyr, though, of course, to the lover they show themselves in addition as brave in adversity, uncomplaining in spite of endless complaints, and true-blue martyrs. The lover in any case has no eyes to see what is being displayed to him under this very thin veil, so all is well.

For such women the younger the lover is the better, because the less unsophisticated, and therefore the less likely to see through the veil. The choice is instinctive to them, just as all their actions and decisions are instinctive; for, deceiving herself just as thoroughly as she deceives her lover, a woman of this type has no idea that she has anything to hide, or why unsophistication better suits her book, or indeed that she is not everything she pretends to be.

She lives in a world of pretence. Even her inflammation of the young lover is academic. Such women lack a sense of reality. Exact details of truth do not matter to them so long as the effect produced is what they feel to be the right one. It would never have occurred to Mrs. Rattenbury, just as it probably never occurred to Mrs. Thompson, that with the less complex-minded young male, feelings are the pre-

cursors of action. That a young man should be afire to
avenge her and her wrongs upon the cruel, drunken dummy
of a husband which she has set up, gives this kind of woman
a supreme delight. The idea that he might actually do so in
bloody fact would fill her with genuine horror. This speci-
men of feminine psychology at its most incomprehensible
to the masculine mind, has never been estimated by a British court of law at its true value. The French, of course,
understand it thoroughly.

We may be certain, then, that just like an idiot child
playing with fire, Mrs. Rattenbury deliberately inflamed
Stoner's already considerable jealousy, still only with the
idea in her foolish mind of increasing his affection for herself; for it is an axiom with such women that the greater the
jealousy the greater the love. With the devilish instinct of
her type, she would have showered attentions on her husband in the presence of her lover: attentions which she would
not have bestowed on him had the lover been absent. If
Stoner were not there, she would say a careless good-night
to Mr. Rattenbury as he sat in a drunken semi-coma. If she
knew Stoner was watching through the window she would
kiss her hardly-conscious husband, ruffle his hair affection-
ately, address him by pet-names, and all the rest of it.

There seems to be two or three unconscious causes for
this instinct. Such women delight in taunting their lovers,
not by word but by action, with the unofficial nature of their
position, and therefore with its precariousness. They delight
in inflicting the pain of seeing the attentions which the lover
covets for himself alone, bestowed elsewhere. They delight
in reminding the lover that they are tied and bound, the
helpless possessions of their husbands, that their horrid situation requires certain duties of them, and that repugnant
as those duties may be, as honourable women they are determined to carry them out, at the cost of anybody else's
feelings; and finally, with a truly damnable perversity they
delight in showing their lovers that they are jolly well fond
of this dear old gross brute of a husband of theirs, and the

lover can lump it or leave it—in other words, they are not completely won yet.

Of course these women do not consciously realize why they do all this, or even why it delights them. They seldom act consciously at all. And though their minds are concerned almost exclusively with themselves and their own affairs (even their generosity, when they are generous, is often only another cause for self-glorification and praise), they are quite incapable of seeing through the fog of their own spreading to the real, selfish, petty core within.

This is exactly the way in which Mrs. Thompson behaved towards Bywaters, and a French judge and jury would have understood at their real value, which was nil, such absurd statements in her letters as that she had been feeding large pieces of glass to her husband in his food and it had done him no harm at all. To take them as literal fact was a piece of stupidity just as crass as that of Mrs. Thompson in making them.

We are justified, therefore, in assuming that this is the treatment which Mrs. Rattenbury accorded to Stoner, but in Mrs. Rattenbury's case there was another factor of the first importance, and that was the greater discrepancy in age. Any woman in Mrs. Rattenbury's situation must remain only too conscious of the difference in age between herself and a lad literally young enough to be her son; and she will be impelled to counter it by making herself more interesting and still more interesting to her lover. With a normal woman these efforts take the natural and harmless forms of affection and passion, intelligence, physical endurance, and the like. In the case of a woman of the neurotic, ego-centrical type, already bent on making herself important, the appeal will be made for pity. She is in any case full of self-pity already, so the material is all ready to hand.

Now pity carries with it the corollary of resentment. To pity the individual we must resent either circumstances or another person who had brought the victim into such a plight. Mrs. Rattenbury, then, like any other wife of this

type, could only rouse pity for herself by causing resentment against her husband. That she had cause for resentment, Stoner could see with his own eyes. Mr. Rattenbury
was a drunkard; he was mean when sober; he had actually
used physical violence on his wife. His only virtues were
his impotence and his complacence as regards Stoner, neither of which was admirable. So much Stoner could see,
and we may be sure that Mrs. Rattenbury added detail after
detail of a highly intimate nature, such as Stoner could by
no means have known for himself, with the appalling lack
of reticence which is a sign of her type.

The result is easy to imagine. As Mrs. Rattenbury poured
out, in a wistfully brave voice, this and that grievous tale
of her married life, instinctively exaggerating and even inventing in order to rouse her unsophisticated young lover to
still more fervid heights of pity and love, Stoner, if he had
any decency at all (and his later conduct shows that he had),
must often have boiled over with rage at the thought of this
exquisite, this altogether exceptional woman tied to such a
gross brute. It is a situation, we may repeat, that arises
often enough in each generation, but it seldom leads to murder. Mrs. Thompson was hanged for her share in the ancient
game because, being a genuinely and not a pseudo-
exceptional woman, she played it too well and really did
drive her lover to the extreme step. She was no loss to the
world, for all women of this type are a pest and a nuisance
to society; but the law being what it is, her condemnation
was as improper as that of Mrs. Rattenbury would have
been. (But were the women of England, with their feminine
contempt for letter and precedent, right, then, after all?)

So, during January and February 1935, though we know
there was never any conscious incitement on Mrs. Rattenbury's part to Stoner to do bodily harm to her husband, we
do get a great deal of unconscious incitement, quite apart
from that form of incitement which lay in rousing Stoner's
own greed and ambitions; so that whatever motives of his
own Stoner may have had in wishing Mr. Rattenbury dead,

he must have thought that he had plenty on Mrs. Rattenbury's behalf too.

There is no reason to deny Stoner some share of the higher qualities. We may assume, on the evidence of his jealousy alone, that his feelings for Mrs. Rattenbury, if not particularly noble—certainly nowhere near the plane of Crippen's for Ethel le Neve—were at any rate genuine; and we may believe that if he struck two blows for himself he may yet have thought that he was striking the third for her.

To admit that there was unconscious incitement of Stoner by Mrs. Rattenbury is not, however, the same as to assume that if Mrs. Rattenbury had not been a neurotic type Stoner would never have murdered her husband once he realized that she had fallen desperately in love with him. All we can say is that Mrs. Rattenbury's character probably hurried the tragedy on. But murder comes from within. If it did not, the husbands of all hysterical, feather-brained, self-pitying wives would come to violent ends. Murder depends entirely upon the mentality of the possible assailant: no amount of incitement will produce murder in one case, while in another case half the amount of provocation will bring a Stoner into the dock on the capital charge.

What was there in Stoner, then, that caused him to murder? He was sitting very pretty, with a complacent husband, a wealthy and generous mistress, and none of the material difficulties which usually accompany adultery; he had, for instance, neither the difficulty of access nor the financial problem with which Bywaters had to contend. Why, then, gild the lily with that ha'p'oth of gold-paint which was all that Mr. Rattenbury's death could offer?

It is difficult to find any other answer than that Stoner was a born bad hat. If Mrs. Rattenbury had not fallen in love with him probably the murder would never have taken place. As it was, we may see Stoner during these early months of 1935 with a mind divided: half raging with resentment against Mr. Rattenbury on his mistress's behalf, and half wondering what there might be in it for himself if only Mr. Rattenbury were out of the way. In all likelihood

the visit to London in March made up his mind for him.
He had not enough ballast to stand up under the temptation
of so much unaccustomed luxury, which might be his ever
afterwards if only two conditions could be fulfilled. Stoner
returned from London to Bournemouth loaded with gifts,
and with the knowledge that luxury like this was at Mrs.
Rattenbury's command, that Mrs. Rattenbury was generous, and that Mrs. Rattenbury loved him to distraction—
him, George Stoner, the bricklayer's son. Is it too much to
believe that he returned, too, with the determination, wa-
vering before but now firm, to secure his future while the
pot was still on the boil?

This, at any rate, seems best to explain the various circumstances of this very stupid murder, and to reconcile
those which appear opposed. That the murder was the result
of a plan made between Mrs. Rattenbury and Stoner, which
was the theory of the prosecution, can no longer be maintained; that it was committed in a fit of blind fury and
jealousy, as a retort to the proposed visit to Bridport, which
was the suggestion put forward by Stoner's defence, seems
equally untenable in view both of the evidence of premeditation and the time which elapsed between the provocation
and the deed. But if Stoner had been toying in his mind for
weeks with the notion of how advantageous it would be to
himself if only Mrs. Rattenbury were a widow; if he had
progressed by an easy stage to the more or less nebulous
wish to kill Mr. Rattenbury if the old man could not hurry
up and die; and if he had come back from London with the
decision fully formed to kill Mr. Rattenbury on the first
opportunity that offered—then the pattern begins to take
form.

Stoner wanted to marry Mrs. Rattenbury. That, I think,
is the king-post of the structure. Stoner had assessed Mrs.
Rattenbury's devotion to himself, and he was sure that, if
she were free, she would marry him. His nest would then
be nicely feathered, and he would have to fear neither woman's whims nor any other agency which might plunge him
back into poverty again as easily and as swiftly as he had

been lifted out of it. He would be secure. He would be rich. He would have, with all this wealth, a woman of whom he was exceedingly fond. And, to differentiate him from all the other youths who in similar circumstances would never have dreamed of murder, the inhibition which ought to have been there to restrain him was lacking: he simply did not shudder at the idea of murder. (Stoner's calm behaviour and dozing in the car during the early hours of the morning after the murder had been committed, is clear proof that he lacked the normal civilized person's horror of bloodshed and violent death.)

If this is the truth, the interval between the quarrel with Mrs. Rattenbury and the time of the murder becomes significant. Stoner would have spent it not in calming down, as might have been expected, but in working himself up. "This is my chance!" one can imagine him muttering to himself. "He's asked for it now, and he's going to get it. I *will* do it this time—by God I will!" And the borrowing of the mallet, the donning of gloves, and all the rest of it, just fall into line. Indeed the only thing that remains unexplained is the stupidity which apparently left no possible loophole of escape. But who can say what might not have been in a mind like Stoner's? It is quite on the cards that he really believed that, if a murderer wore gloves and left no finger-prints, he could never be caught. That, or some equally foolish notion, must have been in his thoughts.

It will be noticed that this theory cuts across the general belief that Stoner was dominated by Mrs. Rattenbury, as was taken for granted in court. I do not believe that Stoner was dominated by Mrs. Rattenbury for a moment. In matters of social behaviour and so on, of course, Mrs. Rattenbury had her influence, but when it came to action, Stoner was the predominant partner each time. There is evidence of it. Mrs. Rattenbury tried hard to prevent Stoner from going up to London, ostensibly to buy drugs. She had no success. Over the Bridport incident Stoner was not pleading; he was issuing orders.

Besides, a woman of Mrs. Rattenbury's type does not

want to dominate, except in the mild way of influence: both morally and physically she loves to be dominated. It gives her a thrill. No doubt Mrs. Rattenbury taught and encouraged Stoner to dominate her. The only mistake both of them made was that she was not under his domination so much as they supposed. If Stoner was sure that Mrs. Rattenbury would marry him if he could set her free, Mrs. Rattenbury certainly did not want to do anything of the sort. She was quite satisfied with things as they were. But even so, if Stoner could have executed his plan without ending up in the dock, probably he would have got Mrs. Rattenbury to the altar quickly enough. As against all this, the only reason which seems to be offered for the assumption that Mrs. Rattenbury was the dominant one of the two, is that she was so much older, which, as many young men and older women could have told the court, is absurd.

How does murder come about? How does it happen that an apparently decent, even lovable youth can take a mallet and bang a defenceless, drunken old man on the head with it, intending that he shall die?

Well, that is how it comes about. And a community determined upon absolute justice would no doubt make foolishness a crime and, if it hanged the youth who struck the blows, hang equally the foolish woman who made the murder possible. But even there difficulties will arise. What if the youth is a criminal born, who would have gone wrong sooner or later in any case? Is the woman to be expected to discern this? And if she does not do so, is she to be just as culpable for his going wrong sooner instead of later as if she had corrupted with her stupidity a pure white soul?

Perhaps the statute-book is best after all. But what, in that case, is one to make of the condemnation of Mrs. Thompson? We should really make up our minds which variety of justice it is that we are going to administer.

POSTSCRIPTUM

Since the preceding was written, there has been published a full transcript of the trial of Mrs. Rattenbury and Stoner, edited by Miss Tennyson Jesse,[1] in the *Notable British Trials* series. When I undertook to write this account, I understood that this book would be published before the semi-official volume, but owing to certain delays that was not possible, and I am therefore taking the opportunity to add this postscript.

I feel it the more advisable to emphasize that this story of the case was written before Miss Tennyson Jesse's volume appeared, since I find to my mingled pleasure and dismay that in her brilliant introduction not only has Miss Jesse arrived at certain conclusions which are the same as my own and laid emphasis on identical points, but that we seem sometimes to have hit upon identical phrases for doing so. (For instance, we both remark on Mrs. Rattenbury's "bad taste" in receiving her lover in a room where her small son was sleeping.) So, as the second arrival on the scene, I must defend myself against any possible suspicion of too obvious an inspiration.

It would be as well perhaps to explain at the same time that my account of the case was based entirely on the newspaper reports, which, of course, are not full, and was written without reference to any of those who played a part in the proceedings. Miss Tennyson Jesse, on the other hand, has consulted and talked with many of those who were called as witnesses, and she has therefore a great deal more information than ever appeared in the newspapers. Some of this information that she publishes clears up certain questions which were bothering me.

After consideration I have decided to leave my account of the case exactly as I wrote it, and just deal here with a few of the doubtful points.

[1] *The Trial of Alma Victoria Rattenbury and George Percy Stoner.* Edited by F. Tennyson Jesse. Wm. Hodge and Co., Ltd. 10*s*. 6*d*.

For instance, with the full report of the trial before me I
see that certain questions were asked about the possible
erection of a tent or shelter in the garden for which Stoner
might have wished to use a mallet, but the main conclusion
is not altered, for it was made obvious that no such tent or
shelter was to have been put up. The period of premeditation is therefore only confirmed.

From Miss Tennyson Jesse's inquiries certain interesting
items emerge. Mrs. Rattenbury, for example, was the
daughter of a printer living, in a poor way, in British Co-
lumbia. Mr. Rattenbury was married when he first met her,
and she was cited in a divorce case which his wife brought
against him. He was then sixty years old and Mrs. Rattenbury thirty-one. It was owing to this scandal that they left
Canada for England when they married.

The occasion on which Mr. Rattenbury gave his wife the
famous black eye was the only time they had a serious quarrel, and when he left the house Mrs. Rattenbury really feared
that he had gone out to kill himself, which was largely why
she sent for her doctor. It was the opinion of Miss Riggs
and others that Mr. Rattenbury really did not know that
Stoner was his wife's lover, although she believed that she
had told him so more or less straightly; but Miss Jesse, after
seeing the Villa Madeira itself, finds this hard to credit.

Stoner always told his counsel that it was he who had
killed Mr. Rattenbury, but for weeks after her arrest Mrs.
Rattenbury was anxious to take the full blame, in spite of
the urgings of her solicitor and counsel. It was only when
her elder son was sent expressly to beg her to tell the truth
in court that she agreed to do so. Miss Tennyson Jesse makes
the interesting point that this is perhaps the only occasion,
when two persons were tried together for one murder, that
"neither of the accused have abandoned the other in a
scramble for safety."

I was not surprised to see that Miss Jesse makes hay of
the ridiculous assumption, made by the judge and both
counsel at the trial, that because of her greater age Mrs.
Rattenbury dominated her young lover. And she quotes a

most interesting and unexpectedly up-to-date letter written by Benjamin Franklin to show that in such cases enlightened opinion will be more ready to believe that it is the young man who dominates the older woman. She makes the further point that it is absurd to pretend, as a court of law always does in this sort of case, that sexual relations are actually physically harmful to a lad of eighteen. Anyone who has been a lad of eighteen once, as presumably even learned judges themselves have, know that this ingenuous theory bears no relation to fact. (The passages concerning this point were not reported in the newspapers.)

Another small point which was not clear to me was that the Central Police Station in Bournemouth took no less than half an hour to send a police-officer after the doctors had reported foul play, which is certainly very different from what we are led to believe in detective stories. Also the situation which seemed so dramatic of Miss Riggs and Stoner left alone together at the Villa Madeira after Mrs. Rattenbury's arrest, was actually made a good deal more prosaic by the presence of Miss Riggs' mother and brother, who moved in to stay with her there on the day of Mrs. Rattenbury's arrest until after that of Stoner. Miss Jesse also clears up the rather confused account of the events which led up to Stoner's arrest. Miss Riggs, it seems, had a talk with the doctor, in which she averred that, although Stoner had confessed his guilt to her, she could not bring herself to divulge to the officials the secret of Mrs. Rattenbury's liaison with Stoner. The doctor, however, persuaded her that, when a life is at stake, a matter of moral reputation is rather small beer, and Miss Riggs thereupon consented to make her statement to the police during the afternoon while Stoner was in London. Stoner was then arrested on his return to Bournemouth the same evening.

Miss Jesse animadverts, as any humane person must, upon the dreadful smugness with which an adulterous woman is always treated in an Anglo-Saxon court, and I notice that we picked out the same sentence of the judge's for comment. As she very truly says, "There are some of us . . . who are so constituted that we cannot see a fellow-human in the extreme of remorse, shame and despair, without feeling pity as well as disgust.'' One cannot emphasize this too much. As I ventured to hint myself, there was One who did not feel even disgust. As for what Mr. Justice Humphreys said of this wretched, silly woman, ''more,'' comments Miss Jesse drily, ''could hardly be said of George Joseph Smith, or of a systematic poisoner, or a baby-farmer.'' This is sadly true, but our judges must, presumably, suit their official remarks to the public, and it is the public who must take the blame. As Mrs. Rattenbury's own counsel repeated: ''Let him that is without sin cast the first stone.'' And yet there are many, many who have that stone in their hands, ready for casting. Ready? Who have already cast it! One envies them their self-satisfied rectitude.

Are they perhaps those same persons on whose behalf the gentlemen of the Press are forced to go to such repulsive lengths? Was it to satisfy the beastly curiosity of these very stonethrowers, wallowing in the slough of their own smugness, that Mrs. Rattenbury was, to all practical purposes, hounded to her death by reporters? Every decent citizen should be grateful to Miss Jesse for printing the story. It cannot be repeated too often, so that the readers of the lower Press may learn what is being done, advisedly or not, on their behalf.

After her acquittal these carrion-crows gave Mrs. Rattenbury no quarter. They besieged the flat where she was trying to hide. When she was taken to a nursing-home by a doctor they pursued her, shouting, ''If you take her to Bournemouth, we'll follow you.'' There can be little doubt that they finally unhinged an already loosened mind. In the pathetic fragments of notes that she left behind her, Mrs. Rattenbury referred to their persecution of her. And if this persecution had been questioned, the reply would have been: ''Our readers demand it.'' One day, perhaps, a reporter of the gutter-Press, in a fit of decent feeling will murder the proprietor who gives him his orders, and then we shall have a trial worth hearing.

On one point only, I think, do I find myself at variance with Miss Jesse. She plainly finds it difficult to account for Stoner's crime, and possibly she avoids the issue when she sets it down to "infantilism . . . an adolescent urge to heroics . . . a gesture conceived in an unreal world". It may be true that "our prisons are full of sufferers from infantilism, and what goes on in their heads bears no relation at all to real life", but I cannot feel that Stoner's action is to be explained quite so easily. Where personal advantage looms so large if a certain person can only be knocked out of the path, the consequent knocking-out bears a very solid relation to real life.

Those who wish to study this extremely interesting case at first hand and form their own opinions thereon, will be well advised to peruse the trial itself. It makes absorbing reading, and it is not too much to say that Miss Tennyson Jesse's penetrating and succinct essay which prefaces it may well become a criminological classic.

F.I.

PART III

A New Zealand Tragedy

by Freeman Wills Crofts

To ALL STUDENTS of criminology the Lakey Murder Case in the North Island of New Zealand must ever remain one of the most notable on record. It had all the qualities to make it so. A brutal double murder by a clever but callous criminal; a plausible theory set forth by the murderer to account naturally for the facts and so avoid the arousing of suspicion; detective work of an extremely high order, involving persevering research, precise observation and deduction, magnificent team work and the use of the latest scientific methods; and finally a trial at which an overwhelming case was presented, though with the utmost fairness to the accused.

Ruawaro, the region in which took place this terrible crime, is situated some 75 miles south of Auckland and 14 from Huntly. It is in the base of that long peninsula which stretches from the square block of the island for some 250 miles towards the northwest. It is a remote area of rolling hills and valleys, of ridges and gulleys, and of lakes and swamps. Farming is the only industry, though there are allied factories, such as creameries. Life as judged by English standards is hard and somewhat primitive, but the settlers are gradually improving their holdings and making them more comfortable and homelike.

Previous to the tragedy relations between the various inhabitants were on the whole excellent, though there naturally occurred those occasional bickerings inevitable in all such small communities.

Samuel Pender Lakey and his wife, Christobel Lakey, the victims of this abominable murder, were a middle-aged couple living alone and supporting themselves by running a small dairy farm. This meant grinding hard work and but little profit, but the Lakeys made the best of things and were a happy and contented couple. They were good neighbours and were generally liked and respected in the district. It is true that they had had some disagreements with their neighbour, William Alfred Bayly, but these were of a minor type and there seemed nothing to suggest that the peace of the neighbourhood was about to be broken.

Events, however, proved that this was a superficial view. Though to all outward observation everything was moving normally, beneath the surface evil passions were alive. These grew till they blossomed into action. On Sunday, October 15, 1933, occurred the horrible crime which became known as the Lakey Murder Case.

In order better to understand what took place, it may be well to consider certain aspects of the work of a normal day in the Lakey household. As has been said, the couple lived alone and did all the work of their farm themselves.

They owned some thirty cows, and the first job in the morning was their milking. This began at five or earlier, and occupied about three hours. During the morning, also, cream from the previous milking, which had been separated overnight, was filled into cream cans and taken by Lakey on a horse-sledge down to the road at the bottom of his ground, where it was called for by the dairy factory lorry. A point which became of importance later was the position in which Lakey left his cans. He always placed them on the edge of the bank at the side of the road, so that the lorry driver by drawing close in could swing them aboard without climbing down off the lorry.

The day was spent in work of various kinds until the

afternoon. The couple then had tea and Mrs. Lakey prepared supper, the heavy meal of the twenty-four hours. Between tea and supper came the evening milking. The cows were brought in again to the shed by Lakey, while his wife got ready the various tins and pails required. Both the Lakeys milked, and when the work was done Mrs. Lakey returned to the house with some of the milk. Lakey then turned the cows out into a paddock and followed his wife to the house with the remainder of the milk. They then had supper.

Such was the Lakeys' routine, and on that dreadful Sunday of the tragedy they carried it out normally until the afternoon. What then took place was only gradually learnt as a result of the police inquiry.

About 4.15 on that afternoon Mrs. Stevens, a neighbour of the Lakeys, noticed the husband and wife driving their cows towards their cowshed for milking, as they always did at that hour. She did not of course see the actual milking, but looking out again later she realized that it must have been completed, as the cows were then in the paddock in which they were usually kept during the night.

It was the Stevens' as well as the Lakeys' custom to milk their cows again in the early morning, and at about five o'clock, as Mr. and Mrs. Stevens milked theirs, they noticed that the Lakey cows were still in the paddock. The Stevens were surprised at this, as the Lakeys always carried out their work punctually. However, they supposed some trifling delay had taken place, and thought no more of the matter.

About 8.15 Mr. Stevens happened to look out again and saw the cows were still there. It was at once evident to him that something was wrong, so he called another neighbour, a Mr. Wright, and suggested going over to the Lakeys' to investigate.

When the two men reached the house they shouted in through the door to know if anyone were there. Receiving no answer, they went on to the cowshed, where they supposed the Lakeys had gone about the milking. But this place

also was deserted. It was obvious from the condition of the
shed and cows that the milking on the previous evening had
been completed normally, but that no milking had been done
that morning.

Now really uneasy, Stevens and Wright returned to the
house and entered. They found no trace of the Lakeys. They
had evidently not been there since the previous evening as
the bed had not been slept in and the fire had not been
lighted. Afternoon tea had obviously been their last meal,
as the remains of it still stood on the table, but they had not
had supper, the food for which was standing in saucepans
on the cold stove.

That something serious had taken place could no longer
be doubted, and Wright went to the nearest telephone and
reported the circumstances to the police at Huntly. He then
returned to the Lakeys' and began with Stevens to milk the
cows.

In one way or another the tidings spread, and soon some
half-dozen neighbours had assembled at the Lakeys' and
had started a search for the missing couple.

They were presently joined by two constables. When the
details had been told to these officers a more systematic
examination of the premises was undertaken. But nowhere
was there a trace of either of the Lakeys.

Matters were in this state when there came a shout from
another of the searchers, a man named Slater. Not far from
the house was a duck-pond, and it was from there that Slater
called. The others hurried down.

At the edge of the pond and protruding a short distance
into the water was a heap of old manure bags or sacks.
Slater had lifted one of these and beneath it had found a
dead body.

The remaining sacks were quickly removed and it was
seen that the body was that of Mrs. Lakey. She was lying
face downwards with her head in the water and her legs on
the bank. The sacks had evidently been arranged to hide
the remains.

The body was lifted out. It immediately became clear that

the unhappy woman had been dead for some time as the frame was stiff.

Here at last was justification of the neighbours' fears. The arrangement of the sacks precluded the possibility of accident or suicide. With a case of murder to be dealt with the constables at once took more energetic measures. The body was carried into the house and a doctor and a force of detectives were sent for.

An examination of the remains revealed cuts on the chin, above the left eye and on the right elbow. Further medical investigation showed that death had occurred from drowning. The immediate suggestion was that Mrs. Lakey had been struck on the chin and knocked senseless, that her body had then been laid in the duck-pond with the face below the water, and that she had there died.

So much seemed clear, but it left the affair as a whole a greater mystery than ever. There remained the question of the whereabouts of Lakey, as well as the apparently insoluble problems of who had killed Mrs. Lakey and with what motive.

In the afternoon of that day Detectives Allsopp and Snedden arrived from Auckland and took charge of the investigation.

This was conducted on three main lines. First there was the search for Lakey, alive or dead; second, the taking of innumerable statements from neighbours and others who might have come in contact with the couple; and third, a detailed search of the premises and surroundings for physical clues.

In the first of these efforts, the hunt for Lakey, the neighbours turned out in strength to assist the police. The country was difficult. Surrounding the little settlement were lakes and swamps in which a body might lie hidden almost indefinitely. In circles of ever-growing radii, with the Lakey home as centre, the search proceeded.

The only place which was not thoroughly examined was the adjoining lake, and that because of the difficulty. It was large in size, and as the bottom was covered with weed, dragging on any scale would have been out of the question. The edge, however, was minutely inspected and no trace was discovered of anything having been thrown in.

On this day the first coherent theory of what might have taken place was put up by the neighbour already mentioned, William Alfred Bayly. He suggested that when walking close to the duck-pond Mrs. Lakey had had a fit and fallen into the pond, injuring her chin and eyebrow, and that Lakey had then found her and been terrified lest he should be suspected of her murder. So frightened had he been that he had lost his head and made a bolt for safety, covering the body with the sacks to postpone discovery and so give him as long a start as possible.

The police had already had this theory in their minds, as well as the more obvious one that Lakey had murdered his wife and fled. They had therefore arranged for the search for the missing man to be carried on throughout the entire country.

At the same time one fact had come to light which suggested to them that the truth might be something different from either of these theories. In searching the house it had been discovered that a brown suit of Lakey's and a pair of boots were missing. The suit was one of Lakey's best, and so far the disappearance of these articles lent colour to the idea of a voluntary departure. But further inquiry revealed an interesting point. The boots were not Lakey's boots at all.

It seemed that a Mr. Gilmour, a friend of the Lakeys, whose farm was approached by means of an unmade clay road, had formed the habit of leaving a pair of his boots at the Lakeys' house, so that when going into Huntly he could travel clean shod. He wore an old pair down his own muddy road, changed them at the Lakeys', and changed back to the muddy ones on his return. It was these boots of Gilmour's which had disappeared.

The police argued that if Lakey had gone off voluntarily he would have worn a pair of his own boots. It seemed to them that the fact that Gilmour's had been taken might indicate that a plant had been staged by someone who did not

know of Gilmour's practice. If this were true it would probably mean that Lakey had been murdered, presumably by
Mrs. Lakey's assailant. While, therefore, all inquiries as to
the man's whereabouts were pushed on, an open mind was
retained as to what had really happened.

The second line of inquiry, the taking of statements from
the neighbours, produced a considerable amount of information. Little of it was, however, at first recognized as
relevant, though afterwards the importance of a good deal
was realized. It may be more convenient to summarize this
information here, rather than give the items in the disjointed
sequence in which they were learnt by the police.

There was, first of all, the matter of the cream cans.

It should be understood that the various farmers left their
separated cream on the side of the road opposite their farms
for collection by the factory lorry, and that Lakey always
placed his near enough the edge of the bank to enable the
lorryman to swing the cans aboard without leaving the ve-
hicle. But on the fatal morning, while Lakey's cans were
there as usual, they were placed a little farther back, with
the result that the lorryman had to get off the van and climb
up on the bank to bring them forward.

This again suggested foul play to the detectives. It looked
as if the cans had been placed on the bank by someone other
than Lakey, someone who knew his habits in general, but
not in complete detail.

A second fact which became revealed was that the un-
pleasantness between the Lakeys and Bayly had been more
serious than was at first realized. It will be remembered
that Bayly was the man who put forward the theory that
Mrs. Lakey had had a fit at the duck-pond and that Lakey
had left the district lest he should be accused of her murder.

All the same the friction did not seem of great importance to the police, particularly as Bayly made no attempt
to hide it. In fact he mentioned it to one of the constables,
saying, "I suppose you already know that we were not on
friendly terms."

The first dispute was about meat. Some sheep of Bayly's

were not thriving on his own land. He obtained permission from Lakey to graze them on the latter's ground on condition that in return Bayly should supply him with a certain quantity of meat. They quarrelled about the carrying out of this bargain.

Apparently there were other causes of disagreement. One day a visitor to the Lakeys named Baldick overheard the two men threatening each other. "If you come on to this farm," said Bayly, "I'll attack you." On another occasion Bayly said of Lakey in the presence of a farmer named Stent, "I would shoot him if he came down here." On still another occasion Stent remarked to Bayly that he was not too friendly with the Lakeys, and Bayly answered, "Yes, I wish I could cause a row with all the neighbours and get them out of it."

A more serious dispute occurred about a road which Bayly wished to make to his farm. This would have involved cutting an opening through Lakey's boundary fence. Bayly asked Stent to go with him when he approached Lakey on the matter so that he might have a witness of the interview. On hearing the request Lakey refused to allow his fence to be cut. High words ensued, and in the presence of three independent witnesses Mrs. Lakey cursed and swore at Bayly, ending up by calling out: "Your bloody guilty conscience is pricking you. You murdered Elsie Walker and we expect the same!" To this Bayly replied, "You won't see the next season out, Lakey!"

The reference made by Mrs. Lakey was to a case which had taken place some five years earlier. A girl, Elsie Walker, had been found murdered. Bayly was undoubtedly acquainted with her and her people, but there was no evidence whatever that he was guilty of the crime. The murderer, in fact, was never found.

In these disputes, none of which appeared very serious, there was no doubt that that bad feeling was mutual.

Another fact which came out as a result of the detectives' inquiries was related by a Miss Kenn, a visitor to the Lakeys. She said that as a Christmas present she had given her host a cigarette lighter. When its original wick was used up Lakey had replaced it with a home-made one of white wool, which he had obtained from his wife's work-basket. Here again it was not till later that the importance of the matter was realized.

There was next the question of firearms. Most of the farmers kept firearms which they used to shoot the wild fowl that abounded in the swamps, as well as rabbits and other game. From various witnesses it was learnt that Lakey had no less than four guns in his house. Of these, one double-barrelled shotgun and a pea-rifle had disappeared at the time of the tragedy.

There was, in addition, a considerable amount of testimony on various other matters relevant and irrelevant which need not be mentioned in this brief summary of the case.

While the search for Lakey was going on and statements were being taken from neighbours, an examination of the site for physical clues was not being overlooked.

In the Lakeys' house nothing of further interest was discovered. Nor was anything more found at the duck-pond. The entire ground surrounding it had been trampled by so many people since the discovery of the body that no individual footprints could be identified.

The search passed from Lakey's ground to that of his neighbour, Bayly, and there some traces of the recent passage of a sledge were observed.

These traces were followed as far as they could be seen. They were found to come from the private road to Bayly's house, go down close to a certain telephone-pole in the boundary fence separating Bayly's and Lakey's properties, turn there in a semi-circle and return to the private road. The suggestion was that something had been carried from Bayly's house to the boundary fence or *vice versa*. The gauge or width between the traces was carefully measured and the trace was pegged off for future reference.

On the following morning the first real clue to what had taken place was discovered.

A large wattle tree stood on Lakey's ground close to the same boundary fence between his ground and Bayly's which

has just been referred to. It was opposite and close to the
telephone-pole near which the traces of the sledge had been
found. Beneath this wattle tree stood a pair of old cartwheels with part of the decaying frame of the cart still attached. In the ordinary course of the examination these
cartwheels came in for close inspection.

At once it was noticed that portions of the surface of the
woodwork had been sliced or pared away, apparently recently. Near these cuts or scrapings some dark marks attracted the detectives' attention, and with suddenly increased
interest they saw that they were bloodstains. A number of
drops of congealed blood were found on the centre and side
of the frame and on the axle.

Some excellent detective work followed. The stains were
first protected to preserve them for later examination and a
meticulous inspection of the wheels was made.

It was then noticed that they bore marks of fresh poultry
droppings.

Now there were no poultry near the wattle tree, Lakey's
hens keeping up close to his house. The question therefore
arose as to whether or not the wheels had recently been
moved to where they were now lying.

The officers raised the wheels and at once saw that they
had. The grass on which they were standing was fresh and
green.

The next step was obvious: Could they find out where
they had come from?

Their efforts on this point were successful. They were
able to find the traces the wheels had made in passing over
the grass. These traces were the only ones in the paddock
and they ran back from near the boundary fence and
telephone-pole to a point close to Lakey's house. Where
they had passed over cow droppings they were clearly visible. The tracks were pegged for reference and the cow droppings removed and packed so as to be available as exhibits
at a future trial should such materialize.

Verbal inquiries were at once instituted into the points

raised by this discovery and it was found possible to settle within limits the time at which the wheels had been moved.

There was plenty of evidence that they had lain for years close to the fence immediately surrounding Lakey's house and had been part of an old cart which had gradually decayed away till only these wheels and axle and centre bar were left. There was definite testimony that they had been in this position on October 11th, that is, four days before the crime. On the morning after the crime they were seen to be under the wattle tree.

The wheels, the sacks which had covered Mrs. Lakey's body, the marked cow droppings, and several other objects were then packed and sent to Auckland for more detailed examination.

That the police were on the track of a premeditated double murder now seemed certain, as owing to the boundary fence being in a different direction, the wheels obviously had not been used to convey Mrs. Lakey's body to the duckpond. The suggestion that they had carried her husband was strong, but in this theory there was a rather overwhelming difficulty. If it were true, where was the body? There seemed to be no possible place about Bayly's farm in which it could have been hidden.

But the fact that the trail of the wheels from Lakey's approached the boundary fence on Lakey's side close to where that of the sledge had gone on Bayly's ground was, however, so suggestive that the detectives decided that a special search of Bayly's farm was called for. They therefore obtained a search warrant and went over. They met Bayly outside his car shed.

Without producing the warrant they asked him if anyone had been near his boundary with a sledge. Bayly at first said no, but afterwards added that when he was returning from taking his cream cans down to the road for collection on the Monday morning, which he did on his sledge, he had noticed the telephone-pole on the boundary fence was leaning over and he had driven up to it to see if it were broken. This, if true, would have accounted for the tracks found. But doubt was thrown on the statement by the fact that when the detectives later examined the pole they could find nothing whatever wrong with it.

Bayly then asked the police if they would care to have a look into his car shed. They did so, but without finding anything of interest. Chief Detective Sweeny, who had been sent for on the discovery of the blood marks on the wheels, then produced his warrant. The search at once began, Bayly raising no objection.

In due course the officers came to examine Bayly's sledge. They measured it and found that its runners corresponded to the trail which had been found, though since Bayly's statement there had been little doubt that it had made the marks. But they found something less expected and more sinister. On some of the top boards were bloodstains. They asked Bayly if they might take three of these boards for examination, and again he raised no objection.

But this was not the only discovery of importance made that day. While Chief Detective Sweeny and his staff were at Bayly's, another constable was searching Lakey's implement shed. There, on a billet of wood he found traces of recent blood.

At once a more detailed search of the shed was undertaken and certain very significant indications were come on.

In front of the shed, which here formed part of the fence surrounding the house, was a kerosene case. When this was moved more bloodstains were found. They were on the wooden rail and battens of the wall, as well as on the grass and an adjoining stone.

Here a similar attempt to hide the stains had been made as in the case of the cartwheels. The surface of the wood had been shaved away. But this time it had been done with less care. Some of the bloodstained shavings were still lying on the ground beneath the kerosene case.

The amount of blood on these various objects was considerable. On some of the battens actual streams had run down. The surface which had been shaved seemed to have been covered with blood, as besides showing on the shavings, smears and spots were visible all round the area.

The rail, battens, shavings, certain blades of grass, and the stone—everything which bore traces of the blood—were removed by the police and sent into Auckland. There they were examined by Dr. Gilmour, pathologist at the Auckland Hospital, as well as by other medical men. They found that all the stains were of human blood.

The indications of what had taken place were growing in number and definition. There was human blood in considerable quantity in the implement shed near Lakey's house, there was human blood on the cartwheels which had recently passed from close to the implement shed to Bayly's boundary fence, and there was human blood on Bayly's sledge, which had recently passed from the same point on Bayly's side of the boundary fence towards Bayly's house. The detectives began dimly to visualize the murder of Lakey in his shed and the transit of the body to Bayly's. There was still, however, the overwhelming difficulty of what had been done with the body.

The search of Bayly's premises was resumed with greater vigour than ever. While it was in progress Detective Allsopp noticed that Bayly was wearing a belt to which was attached a sheath. The handle of the knife in this sheath had been damaged some time previously and looked curious to Allsopp. He asked Bayly if it was a file he had in his sheath. Bayly answered that it was a knife, and pulled it out and passed it over. Allsopp saw that it was ground to a razor edge, except near the shaft, where the edge had been slightly turned.

The search in Bayly's house was continued on the following day with further startling results. In the bathroom was found bloodstained clothing of Bayly's, a shirt with marks on the front and a coat stained on the sleeves. These were taken possession of.

Bayly was asked if he could account for the blood. He said he had cut his finger a few days previously, which might explain it. Also that he had been at a recent calving and might have got spattered.

His hands were then examined and two small cuts were found on one finger. These, however, seemed too old to fit in with his statement, though of this the detectives could not be certain.

In the bathroom were also found Bayly's belt, sheath and pouch. The knife was missing and Bayly was asked where it was. For answer he went to the kitchen and produced it from a cupboard. He raised no objection to handing these articles over, and all four of them—knife, belt, sheath and pouch—were added by the officers to their collection.

In the wash-house were two pairs of dungaree trousers, and Bayly was asked which pair he was wearing on the day of the murder. He replied that it was one of those pairs, though he could not say which. On one of them there were dark stains which looked like blood. Both pairs were also taken by the detectives.

While the trousers were being examined an empty pea-rifle cartridge fell from one of the pockets. Bayly was questioned about this also. He said that he had been shooting on the previous Friday and Saturday and must have dropped the shell into his pocket. "Where is your rifle?" he was next asked. He led the detectives to the separator-room in his cowshed, where the rifle was standing. There were marks like bloodstains on the barrel. These Bayly attributed to a hare which he said he had shot.

In due course all the bloodstained articles were examined by Dr. Gilmour in Auckland. He found that there were several spots of human blood on the trousers. On the rifle there was blood, but it could not be identified as human. There was no blood on the belt, sheath or pouch. But, perhaps the most significant of all the finds, in the thumb hollow on the blade of the knife there was human blood.

In the meantime the general search for Lakey was being pushed on with great energy. For miles in every direction rivers, lakes and swamps were inspected and were dragged in likely places. Over fifty police were engaged at one time, as well as numbers of adjoining residents. As a result of a suggestion that the body might have been burnt in a heap of burning slack at the Renown mill, a squad of constables shovelled over the entire glowing mass. Railways, ports, and shipping were watched in the whole of the two islands. Hospitals and mental homes were visited. Finally, a reward of £100 was offered for information which would lead to the man's discovery, alive or dead.

Then a statement of Bayly's introduced a fresh complication into the affair.

One evening he called on the detectives, who had made Lakey's house their headquarters, to say that a man and dog had been trespassing on his ground shortly before. He had surprised them about his car shed. The man had taken to his heels and had got away, but Bayly's dog had caught and held the other dog.

Bayly then declared that the dog belonged to his neighbour, Mr. Wright. To the police he said he did not know who the man was, though afterwards he hinted that it must have been Wright.

The detectives made inquiries and satisfied themselves that it could not have been Wright, as he was able to prove he was at home at the hour in question. They could not discover the identity of the man, or indeed whether any man had been there at all.

Some days later Detective Allsopp commenced a more detailed and systematic search of the swamps and waterholes on Lakey's and Bayly's farms. They had been inspected already, but not in his opinion with sufficient care. These waterholes were full of soft black mud, covered with slime and water. The new method of search was to probe them inch by inch with spades and spears.

By that Monday afternoon the searchers had reached a hole some 140 yards from Bayly's house, not far from where the cartwheels and sledge traces had been found. There a constable's spear struck metal.

He reached down beneath the water and drew the object out. It proved to be the barrels of a double-barrelled shotgun, and was bright and free from rust. Close by in the same waterhole was the fore end of a shotgun. In another hole at a little distance was the stock of a pea-rifle.

The officers replaced these objects in the swamp, noting

their positions. Then they brought Bayly down. When he
saw the spot to which he was being taken, he showed considerable surprise. The detectives pulled out the articles one
by one and asked Bayly if they were his. He replied that
they were not, that he did not hide them and that he had no
idea how they came to be there.

Search in the swamp continued, and later in the day the
barrel of a pea-rifle was discovered. This fitted the stock
previously found. The stock of the double-barrelled shotgun, however, was still missing, when owing to the dusk
the officers had to knock off work.

That night a watch was put on the swamp lest an attempt
to remove further hidden articles should be made.

About ten o'clock the two constables in charge saw Bayly
leave his house and approach down the hill. They lay down
silently and watched. They were satisfied that they could not
be seen as they were dressed in dark clothes and were hidden
in an old pit. Bayly came close to the swamp, then stopped
and looked cautiously round in every direction. Then he moved
silently on towards where the guns had been found.

When he reached the edge of the water the constables called
out to him. Bayly looked round and said that it was all right
and that he had seen them. This, however, the constables were
satisfied was false. Bayly then returned to his house.

Next day the searchers came on the missing shotgun stock
belonging to the double barrels already found. These discoveries now made up two complete weapons, a double-
barrelled shotgun and a pea-rifle.

It will be remembered that a double-barrelled shotgun
and a pea-rifle were missing from the Lakeys' house. It was
natural to suppose that these were the same. The police
therefore examined the gun licences in question and found
that they were.

The evidence which was slowly being amassed was
pointing more and more definitely in one direction. But there
was still nothing of certainty in it. Now, however, a fresh
discovery was made, which though it scarcely provided sufficient proof for court, banished all doubts as to the author

of the crime from the minds of the investigators. This discovery was made at headquarters and was an outstanding triumph for use of scientific methods in detection.

Sergeant Dinnie, of the Criminal Registration Department at Wellington, was a finger-print expert and an adept at photographic work of all kinds. He was sent by Auckland to examine the exhibits and see whether he could suggest any development from the use of his speciality. He thought he could, and determined to try some experiments.

First he took one of the pieces of timber from Lakey's implement shed which had been pared or shaved, and of it made an enlarged photograph, using a magnification of eight and a half diameters. It showed fine ridges or scrapes due to irregularities in the edge of the knife. He cut the photo across in the centre at right angles to the direction of these ridges.

Then he took Bayly's knife and made a similar enlargement of its edge. This had to be done in nine sections, and when the sections were joined it made a strip some four feet long. The edge showed irregularities of the same type as those on the wood.

An interesting operation followed. The sergeant placed the two photographs together so that that of the wood scrapes was applied to that of the edge of the knife. Slowly he moved the former along the latter. And then suddenly he was rewarded for his trouble. At one point ridges and furrows exactly coincided!

Further examination and photographs of wood and knife were made under a magnification of ten diameters. These were checked by Dr. Dennis Brown of Auckland University College. He also carried out independent tests of a similar kind and these fully confirmed Dinnie's conclusions.

No doubt that Bayly had murdered Lakey now remained in the minds of the detectives, but the evidence against him was still far from complete. In the case of Lakey, failure to produce the body would make a charge of murder impossible, while there was no proof whatever that Bayly was concerned in Mrs. Lakey's death. Further investigation was required.

Under these circumstances it was decided to search Bay-

ly's homestead once again. And this time discoveries were
made which at last gave a clue to the ghastly truth and led
to an overwhelming case being presented at the trial.

When examining Bayly's cowshed some days before this,
the detectives had noticed a shovel bearing some deposit
that looked like ash. They asked Bayly what this was and
he said he did not know. The officers then said they would
take the shovel for examination. Bayly, however, objected
on the ground that he required it to carry on his work. The
officers agreed to leave it, but they scraped off the deposit
and sent it to Auckland with their other exhibits. It had there
been examined and was found to be bone ash, charcoal and
burned sacking.

This was a fact heavy with dreadful suggestion. It brought
to the detectives' minds certain testimony they had received at
the beginning of the inquiry, testimony which they now began
to think had not been given sufficient attention. One item was
detailed by a neighbouring farmer named Herbert, the second
had been mentioned by many witnesses and indeed was within
the observation of the detectives themselves.

Mr. Herbert had stated that towards dusk on the Sunday
evening of the crime, he had looked down across from his
own farm to that of Bayly. From Bayly's cowshed was pour-
ing a great volume of smoke. He had never seen anything
like it before, and so impressed was he that he called another man named Brooker, and they watched it together. At
times they could scarcely see the shed for the smoke. Off
and on Herbert looked at it until he went to bed some three-
quarters of an hour later. During the whole of that period
the smoke had continued to pour out.

The second item was that on the following day and for
two or three days after, Bayly's eyes were red and sore-
looking, just as might have been expected had he been for
any time in a smoky atmosphere.

The efforts of the officers were now concentrated on a
new line of inquiry: a search for evidence of fires and burn-
ings. It was not long before they found it.

On the ground not far from the cowshed they noticed the

bottom half of a 40-gallon benzine drum. It had obviously been used as a stove, both because of its discoloration and because a square fire hole was cut out of the side. Asked to account for it, Bayly said he had cut the drum in two because it was old and useless and because he wanted the lower half to make a fire in. This fire was for the purpose of warming an iron, and he produced an old axe which showed signs of heat. He said that the upper half of the drum was in the orchard. The detectives took charge of both halves.

It was obvious that Bayly had cut the drum in two recently, for among the original statements which had been made was one concerning it. Different neighbours had mentioned that Bayly had a large copper which he used for boiling water for cleaning and scalding pigs. This until lately had been supported by means of steel slips on the drum. All testified to the fierce heat which could be generated in the contrivance.

The half drum was standing bottom upwards, and the searchers turned it over. On the bottom was a deposit of ash which looked identical with that found on the shovel. This was collect and placed in envelopes. On the floor of the separator-room of the cowshed were suspicious-looking stains, and from these samples were also taken.

Beside the separator-room there was a vessel containing sheep dip. The officers asked if they might empty this vessel, but Bayly objected. "If you empty it," he said, "you will have to take full responsibility if any of the cattle are poisoned." The dip was accordingly left untouched for the time being.

A few minutes later another discovery was made. In a small paddock not far from the house were a number of bones. Bayly was asked what he did with these. "I smash them up and put them in the garden," he answered. "Do you burn them?" the officers asked. Bayly said that he did not.

These investigations could have left no doubt in Bayly's mind as to the direction the inquiry was now taking. The heavy pall of smoke which had hung over the cowshed on the night of the murder was no doubt in his mind as it was in the officers', and it was evident that the cause of this smoke would be investigated with the utmost energy.

Whether or not these considerations weighed with Bayly is a matter of surmise. But he now took a step which immediately changed the character of the investigation, bringing matters at once to a head.

Bayly disappeared.

On the morning of December 1st the officers had occasion to call once again at his house, and it was then that they found he was missing. How in that district filled with police the man had been able to slip away, they didn't know, but all they learnt was that he had been gone several hours before they became aware of the fact.

Mrs. Bayly was questioned and she produced a letter from her husband. It was dated for the previous day and read:

                                              30/11/33.

My darling Phylly,

   Yesterday in Auckland I received definite information that the police were going to try and put the blame of Mrs. Lakey's death and Lakey's disappearance on to me. They have to vindicate themselves somehow—after the blunders they have been making in the search for Lakey, and think I will be the easiest one to catch. As you know, I was with you that night; but I do not intend to let them put their dirty tricks on me. I have picked out a nice spot to rest in, so love to you and the kids. The farm will bring you in a bit.

                                              Bill

Then ensued a hue and cry! Immediately a warrant was issued for Bayly's arrest, and police circles in the entire island hummed with excitement and activity.

Detective Allsopp was early able to prove that the letter had not been received through the post, but had been written by Bayly before leaving home. He found a pad of similar sheets of which the top one bore the impress of the writing. It seemed probable, therefore, that the letter had been intended for the police rather than the wife, and it was suggested that its object was to convey the idea that Bayly was about to commit suicide.

Whether Bayly had really intended to give the authorities the slip is, however, doubtful, for two days later the police were informed that he was with his solicitor, Mr. Lusk, in a house near Auckland. There they found him and there he was arrested. He was taken to Auckland and lodged in the Central Police Station.

In the meantime the search on his farm was prosecuted with greater intensity than ever. Now attention was turned to the ground itself. Detective Allsopp remembered that on his first arrival he had noticed that a certain area near the house had been freshly dug. As nothing had since been planted at the place, the motive of digging seemed obscure. It was therefore decided to dig over the ground again to make sure that nothing had been buried.

The officers set to work. Scarcely, however, had they gone a yard when they made a discovery which they believed would at long last solve their problem.

Coming up with the earth were bits of charcoal, pieces of burnt bone and grass. It looked as if the bones and charcoal had been emptied on the grass and then been dug in. Immediately the men stopped their rough digging and began to remove the earth with meticulous care, sifting every particle before throwing it aside. Their trouble was rewarded.

Besides many fragments of bone, they came on a clip and stud from a pair of braces, several pieces of cloth, a number of small nails such as are used in bootmaking, and two artificial teeth. All these articles were more or less burnt.

The area of search was then extended. The ground around the cowshed was opened and more pieces of burnt bone were dug up. Burnt bone was also found in the grass in various places. In a toolshed part of the case of a watch bearing a number was come on, and among some old bolts were a few small screws and springs which the searchers thought had come from a cigarette lighter. Different parts of what appeared to be the same watch, damaged as if the watch had been cut in two, were unearthed from various places. The charred stem of a cherry-wood pipe was also found and it was similar to one known to have been in Lakey's possession. From the grass of the orchard near the main house were picked up more burnt bones and rags, the toe-plate of a boot, part of a dental plate bearing a tooth, a trousers button, pieces of material such as is used for men's underpants, and part of a pocket of a pair of trousers.

The vessel of sheep dip was emptied and at the bottom were found more burnt bones and charcoal, the case of a cigarette lighter, and a tuft of hair.

It will give some idea of the amazing comprehensiveness of the search when it is mentioned that *several hundred* pieces of bone were found, and of the meticulous care with which the work was carried out by instancing the discovery of such tiny objects as single artificial teeth in the rough grass of a paddock.

All this vast array of "exhibits" was turned over to the scientists at Auckland, and their work was characterized by equal comprehensiveness and care. The bones were classified into (*a*) those which were too small to be identified, (*b*) those which might be human, but could not be proved to be so, and (*c*) those which were definitely human. Of the latter, pieces of ribs, vertebrae, skull, thigh bone, and others were identified. No less than fifty-five fragments had come from the skull alone.

An attempt was made to reconstruct the frame from which these bones had come. This could not be done in its entirety, but certain conclusions were drawn.

There was no absolute evidence that the deceased had been a man, but the size of the bones and the muscular attachments which were found indicated a strength and build which was probably male. There was, however, no definite proof that the remains were those of a person of middle age. The deduction from the tuft of hair was more convincing. It was found to be human hair, two and a half inches long, coarse, and of a greyish-brown colour. This was almost certainly male, and corresponded exactly to Lakey's hair, both in colour and length.

An important point brought out by the scientists was that the bones had only lately been burnt. This was proved, not only by their freedom from dirt, but from the fact that some of them still bore charred flesh.

The finds other than human were also tests and certain extremely interesting conclusions were reached. Of these, perhaps, the most striking were in connexion with the cigarette-lighter and watch.

The small screws and springs picked out from among some old bolts were found to fit the lighter case taken from the vessel of sheep dip. The case was similar to Lakey's. But there was more. In the case was a home-made wick consisting of wool. It will be remembered that when the original wick was used up, Lakey had put in a new wick from his wife's work-basket. The wool in the lighter and that from Mrs. Lakey's basket were compared and were found to be identical.

The watch which had been cut in two was also shown to be Lakey's. Apart from its general appearance, its number was in the records of a Huntly watchmaker. He had sold it to Lakey. Moreover, the implement with which it had been cut in half was found. In Bayly's shed was a pair of strong shears, on the blades of which were traces of two of the metals of which the watch was made.

The various buttons, clips, artificial teeth, pieces of cloth and of rubber which were found and examined need scarcely be enumerated. It is sufficient to say that all of these were consistent with the theory that it was Lakey's body which had been burnt.

One very suggestive fact may however be mentioned. In or among the human remains were found no less than twenty-one grains of lead. Where had this come from? The detectives had little doubt. They believed it was from a bullet or bullets, and that its presence proved that Lakey had been shot. The assumption certainly worked in with their theory. If the deceased had been shot in his implement shed it would account for the quantity of blood on the wall and floor.

During the general inquiry a detailed investigation was
made into the firearms and shells which had figured in the
affair. These consisted of two shotguns and two pea-rifles
in all, one of each type which were missing from Lakey's
and which were found in the swamp on Bayly's farm, and
the others which were in Bayly's possession. There was also
the empty pea-rifle shell which had dropped from the pocket
of Bayly's dungaree trousers.

Careful experiments by Dr. Dennis Brown and Sergeant
Dinnie brought out a very convincing piece of evidence.
They showed that this shell from Bayly's pocket had been
fired from Lakey's pea-rifle. Dr. Brown fired seventeen
shells from this rifle, and all of them had the same striker
marking as the shell found on Bayly. Enlarged photographs,
some to as much as sixty-eight diameters, demonstrated this
clearly. However, to make the matter even more certain the
police collected all the .22 calibre pea-rifles they could find
in the district—no less than twenty-one. Shells were fired
from all of these and in not one case did the striker mark
resemble that of Lakey's.

The police case by this time had grown extremely convincing, but there was one point in it about which a considerable amount of controversy arose. It was argued in certain
quarters that the theory must be incorrect for the simple
reason that it would be impossible to burn a human body
as it was assumed had been done to Lakey's. Authorities on
the subject were consulted and were found—as is usually
the case—to differ.

As this was fundamental to the case for the prosecution,
a definite conclusion had to be reached. It could only be
done in one way. Certain rather ghastly experiments were
therefore carried out.

A 40-gallon drum, similar to that believed to have been
used by Bayly, was obtained and a fire opening was made
low down in the side, exactly as in the other. This was
arranged as Bayly's was understood to have been, and a fire
of wood was lighted. An old ewe weighing over eleven stone
was shot and was placed head downwards in the drum, to-

gether with a pair of gumboots. The fire was stoked up with wood for an hour and a half and then left to burn itself out.

Next morning it was found that the body was entirely consumed, only burnt bone and charcoal remaining. These bones were similar in appearance to those which had been dug up.

Two other similar experiments were carried out when a large ram and a calf, both weighing about ten stone, were burnt. The calf was not shot, but was killed by chloroform. The results in all three cases were identical.

It was observed that during the experiment heavy black smoke was given out similar to that seen hanging over Bayly's cowshed on the night of the murder. This appeared to come, not from the bodies, but from the rubber boots.

Seldom, surely, has so great a mass of evidence been collected in the course of a single investigation as was here placed at the disposal of the Crown solicitors. Seldom, surely, has the guilt of the accused been so adequately established as was that of Bayly. It is suggested that there had been some dissatisfaction with the achievements of the police in previous cases and that they were here on their mettle. Be that as it may, no unbiased person can consider their work without feelings of admiration.

At last the period of preparation came to an end and the test of the work came. Bayly was brought to trial.

The preliminary hearing before the Auckland magistrates began on January 16, 1934, amid scenes of great popular interest. There were sixty-four witness for the prosecution and two hundred exhibits, and the proceedings occupied ten days. The defence was reserved and the expected verdict was recorded. The accused was committed to the Supreme Court at Auckland for trial at the next session.

On Monday, May 21, 1934, opened under Mr. Justice Herdeman what must surely be one of the most notable trials which has ever taken place in any part of the world. Imagination staggers at its length and complexity. It lasted without a break from the 21st of May till the 23rd of June, twenty-nine days of hearing. There were 77 witnesses and 274 exhibits. To deal with the exhibits alone a highly elaborate cross-indexing system of reference had to be devised and carried out.

The morning of the first day was taken up in preliminaries, and in the afternoon the jurors visited Ruawaro, where they inspected the two holdings and the various sheds and fences about which they were going to hear. On the second day the proceedings proper opened with the address of Mr. V. R. Meredith, counsel for the prosecution.

Mr. Meredith spoke for the entire day. He began by reminding the jury that the responsibility they bore was the gravest that any citizen could be called upon to undertake, and warning them not to allow any preconceived opinions they might have formed from conversations or articles in the Press to operate on their judgment in this grave matter. Then he proceeded to outline the case in detail.

He described the Lakeys, their property, and the country in which they lived, mentioning the duck-pond, the pair of old cartwheels, the cowshed, and other objects. Then he detailed the daily routine of the Lakeys' life, the clothes Lakey usually wore, his cherry-wood pipe, his cigarette lighter with the home-made wick, and the fact that he had a set of false teeth. The relations between the neighbours were then discussed and the history of the quarrel with Bayly given.

Turning then to the actual murder, Mr. Meredith told of the heavy smoke which had been seen over Bayly's cowshed on the Sunday evening, of the cows being noticed in the night paddock on the Monday morning, and the inquiries caused thereby, of the calling in of the police and the discovery of Mrs. Lakey's body in the duck-pond.

The investigation of the police was then detailed: how they had found that Lakey's double-barrelled shotgun and the pea-rifle he had been lent were missing; how Bayly put up to them his suggestion that Mrs. Lakey had fallen into the duck-pond in a fit and that Lakey had fled lest he should be charged with murder; and how they came on their first real clue, the tracks of the sledge. The trail of human blood was mentioned; first, on the implement shed; second, on the wheels and frame taken from Lakey's house; third, on

Bayly's sledge; fourth, on Bayly's trousers; and fifth, on the back of Bayly's knife. Then came the incident of the alleged trespasser and Bayly's suggestion that the man was Wright. With the theory of murder and suicide gone, Mr. Meredith contended, Bayly was attempting to fasten suspicion on Wright. But the attempt failed utterly.

The discovery that the deposit scraped off Bayly's shovel was burnt bone and charcoal, went on Mr. Meredith, was the first clue as to the disposal of Lakey's body. When, following this up, the police took possession of the cut petrol drum, Bayly grew alarmed. It was significant that next day he was missing and had left a letter containing a clear suggestion that he was about to commit suicide.

Mr. Meredith went on to describe the burnt bones, parts of underclothing, metal buttons, leather, boot nails, and other objects which were found.

"Whose remains are these?" he asked. "The evidence would indicate that no other inference could be drawn but that they are those of Samuel Lakey. If these are not the remains of Samuel Lakey, whose are they?"

A description of the method by which it was proved that the bloodstained wood had been shaved with Bayly's knife was also given, as well as the experiments with the guns and shells.

Finally Mr. Meredith summarized the theory of the prosecution concerning the affair. He said it was no part of the Crown's case to prove exactly how the murder was committed. The exact sequence of what happened that night on that lonely ridge would probably never be known. Two of the participants were dead and silent for ever, but there was the evidence to be put before the jury. For the Crown's purpose it was sufficient to establish that one or more murders had been committed, and that the accused was guilty of the commission.

Briefly, the theory of the Crown was that Bayly went to the Lakeys' place just before the Lakeys completed milking and struck Mrs. Lakey on the jaw, knocking her out. When Lakey followed his wife up from the cowshed Bayly shot him, Lakey's blood spattering over the implement shed. It would appear that Lakey was attacked without warning, and

that no struggle took place. Mrs. Lakey was dragged to the
duck-pond by her assailant, and her head was submerged in
the water until she expired.

Lakey's body was put on the wheels and frame and carted
down to Bayly's boundary fence. The wheels could not be
taken through the boundary fence, so the sledge was brought
by Bayly from his own road to the same point to carry the
body. From there it was removed to his cowshed, where it
was promptly burnt in a drum. That this could be done there
was no doubt. The drum Bayly subsequently cut in two and
placed in different parts of the garden.

The smoke of the fire was witnessed by a neighbour,
Herbert, and his workman across the lake, Mr. Meredith
continued. The theory was that Bayly put the body in the
drum and burned it, clothes, boots and all. That same night
at some time he covered Mrs. Lakey's body with sacks in
such a way as not to attract the attention of a passer-by;
planted the guns in his own swamp for subsequent disposal;
put Lakey's cream cans down by the road to prevent inquiry,
and took Lakey's gun and clothes, with a view to setting up
the murder and suicide theory, which he himself promul-
gated the next day.

If inquiry had been postponed until next day there would
have been ample opportunity to have properly disposed of the
guns and the residue of the burning. Detection would then have
been impossible. One thing slipped, and that was that neighbours saw that Lakey's cows had not been milked. From
11 a.m. on the Monday onward Lakey's property and Bayly's
were overrun with police and searching settlers. Bayly was
compelled to get rid of what was yet unhidden at once, and
necessarily in the neighbourhood of his own house.

With a peroration on the duty of the jurors a great speech
ended.

For four weeks witnesses were called, examined, cross-
examined and re-examined, and then Mr. Meredith made
his concluding address to the jury. He submitted that the
evidence proved conclusively that a body had been burnt at
Bayly's farm, that there could be no doubt that this body

was Lakey's because, first, several of the burnt objects found were Lakey's property; second, that there was a trail of blood from Lakey's shed to Bayly's, and third, that no one but Lakey was missing. Finally, he suggested that no one but Bayly could be guilty of the crime.

Bayly was defended by two extremely able counsel, Messrs. Northcroft and Leary, but from the first they had a hopeless task. Nevertheless they put up a brave fight. Their cross-examination of the witnesses was relentless, particularly of the scientific witnesses. They used maps, diagrams, blackboards, and photographs were thrown on a screen by a lantern.

By calling no witnesses they obtained a right to the final word with the jury. Their main line of defence was that the evidence brought forward by the Crown was entirely circumstantial. The position, Mr. Northcroft said, was like a chain whose links led to a certain conclusion. But the jury must remember that if one link in a chain broke, the whole of the remainder were absolutely valueless.

He suggested that several of the essential links put forward by the prosecution were faulty. The most important was that no real evidence of motive had been put forward at all. There was no evidence that Bayly had hated the Lakeys sufficiently to wish to murder them. Further, Bayly had been with a neighbour that Sunday afternoon. He was then in a perfectly normal frame of mind. Could it be supposed that he had suddenly risen up and behaved like a demon? Mr. Northcroft scoffed at the "almost superhuman confidence" of the experts in swearing that certain shells had or had not been fired from certain guns, and suggested that the prosecution had mixed the shells up. He argued that it would have been utterly impossible to have carried a body of the weight of Lakey's on the old cart frame and wheels, as the latter would have given way, and further, that Bayly could not have lifted such a weight across his boundary fence without leaving obvious traces: of which there were none. He declared that had Bayly done what he was accused of he would have been spattered with blood from head to foot. He called attention to the bearing of Bayly and insisted that at no time was it that of a guilty man. It was utterly im-

possible, he urged, that between 4 p.m. on the Sunday and
the following morning Bayly could have performed all the actions with which he was credited. There was, moreover, no
evidence of any kind that Bayly had even seen Mrs. Lakey on
the Sunday afternoon. Her injuries might have been inflicted
by accident. Finally, Mr. Northcroft put up the alternative theory that the crime might have been committed by some third
person, which theory would account for all the proven facts.

On Friday, June 22nd, the jury were again taken to Ruawaro so that they might once more inspect the various
premises in the light of the evidence they had heard.

At last, on Saturday, came the final scenes. The judge's
summing-up occupied some two hours. Immediately afterwards the jury retired. They were absent for 71 minutes and
when they came back all saw that Bayly's fate was sealed. They
brought in a verdict of Guilty, and sentence was at once passed.

William Alfred Bayly was executed at Mount Eden Gaol,
Auckland, on July 20, 1934, a few days after his twenty-
eighth birthday.

Thus ended one of the most remarkable criminal cases
on record.

Leaving now the realms of fact for those of speculation, let
us for a moment look at Bayly's plan. Considering it as we
would the plot of a novel, and apart from all questions of
morals or humanity, let us ask ourselves: How far, as a
plan, was it deserving of success? Was it wrecked by accidents which could not have been foreseen or was it inher-
ently defective? If Bayly had had more luck, or taken other
precautions, would it have succeeded?

Its ingenuity cannot be denied. To make the murder of
Mrs. Lakey and Lakey appear as the murder of Mrs. Lakey
by Lakey was a scheme of a brilliancy approaching genius.
In general the method by which Bayly tried to carry it out
seems also flawless. Mrs. Lakey was murdered in the kind
of way which Lakey might have probably enough employed,
and no attempt was made to hide the crime. An attempt was
admittedly made to delay its discovery, but this was strictly

in accordance with what Lakey would have done were he guilty. Evidence that Lakey had left the district was supplied. He would never have done so in his working clothes. Therefore his good suit and boots were removed. The overwhelming argument for his having so left was not, however, one of clothes or boots. If he had not gone his body would remain. Therefore the body must be destroyed. Hiding it would not do; it might be found. It must be annihilated. And this to all intents and purposes was done.

That Bayly failed in his purpose was apparently not due to any defect in his plan. If its execution had been as good as its conception, he should certainly have succeeded. But its execution was faulty. He came down on details.

He made the mistake of taking Gilmour's boots instead of Lakey's. He made the mistake of leaving the cattle in their night paddock instead of getting them down to the shed. He went wrong in placing the cream cans too far back on the mound at the side of the road. He erred in taking his sledge on to soft ground near the boundary, instead of carrying the body to the road. He overlooked returning the wheels to their former resting-place. He failed to shave off all the bloodstains from the timber and to destroy the edge of his knife and re-sharpen it. He burnt the rubber boots, thus creating a black smoke. And so with several other small mistakes of detail.

It is interesting, if perhaps unprofitable, to ask whether he could have avoided these mistakes? In my opinion, for what it is worth, he could not. Or rather, if he had avoided these, he would have made others just as serious.

He obviously did not know about Gilmour's boots. He did not know, or had forgotten, about the placing of the cream cans. It is very unlikely that he would have had time to deal with the cows. Apart from this, an attempt to do so might have landed him into greater trouble. He might have been seen driving them down. If he hadn't milked them in the shed—which he could not possibly have done—they might have lowed and attracted attention. If he had carried the body to his road instead of putting it on his sledge, his clothes would probably have been much more stained with blood than they were. Perhaps a trail of blood would have been dropped on the ground. Probably, even if he had returned the wheels, the bloodstains on the wood and the tracks on the grass would still have been discovered.

Personally I do not believe it possible for anyone to carry through a complicated crime, as this was bound to be, without leaving traces which could be picked up by careful detectives. It is the simple crimes which are hard to detect. Bayly committed many errors. Probably any one of them alone would have hanged him.

It is interesting also to notice, in spite of what certain critics say, that real crimes do not make good detective stories. In this case the very first discovery of the detectives—the finding of the blood on the wheels and sledge—pointed clearly to the criminal. In a novel such an indication should involve someone other than the criminal, or if it indicated the criminal it should not be given until the last chapter. In real cases there can seldom be the "twist" or surprise at the end so beloved of publishers, editors and readers.

Stories of real crimes move their readers because of the human element, which is usually much more predominant than in an invented puzzle. Conversely, as puzzles, real life stories are left far behind. And there is another difference. Real life stories have an atmosphere of sordidness and evil which is happily absent from almost all detective novels.

NOTE.—The Author acknowledges his indebtedness for information to the files of the *New Zealand Herald*, and to Mr. J. Halket Millar's admirable book *The Bayly Murder Case*, published by Messrs. Gordon & Gotch (Aust.) Ltd. The latter is recommended to those desiring a more complete description of the case.